THE PERFECT POODLE

PUPPY TRAINING GUIDE FOR BEGINNERS FROM HOUSE, CRATE AND SEPARATION ANXIETY TO HEALTH AND CARE AND EVERYTHING IN BETWEEN

HELEN DEVLIN

CONTENTS

INTRODUCTION

P oodles are one of our most beautiful of dog breeds. Their temperament, personality, athleticism and intelligence must be second-to-none.

So much so that we see Poodles crosses everywhere today. Cavapoos, Cockapoos, Maltipoos, Labradoodles, Goldendoodles, Schnoodles, Yorkipoos, Pomapoos, Shihpoos, Shitzpoos, Poochons, Dalmadoodles, Bassetoodles to one of the newest, the Bernedoodles.

There is a reason that the Poodle features so heavily in our dogs today, there are few better specimens of the perfect dog.

Your Poodle has very few health problems to worry about, he is very easy to train and the background to his life is a fascinating tour through history - all the way back to at least the 1200s. I would love to only write the story of the Poodle but the purpose of this book is to help him be happy and for you to enjoy all of the time that you spend with him.

This book covers the early puppy training and all of the things that you need to do to help your puppy settle in and to become a healthy and happy family dog.

Puppy training is generally very similar for most dog breeds. Some suffer more with separation anxiety, some like more exercise and need not just basic training, but a focus on training and some need careful attention to inherent heath weaknesses in the breed bloodline. Understanding where your puppy comes from and what it holds in its genes is, I believe, important too.

Years ago I used to know Poodles, but it wasn't until I got to know a few Cockapoos and a Shihpoo well, that I began to look again at the heart of these breeds - the Poodle. It is one of the best things I have ever done.

If you already have your Poodle, well done! I will be joining you soon. If you are still looking, then you can't make a better choice than a Poodle. If you can't decide on a Standard, Miniature or Toy then I will outline the main differences.

This isn't a book about the breed itself, it is about puppy training but, I believe, understanding your dog is the first step to being a good parent and to help you train your puppy faster and better. I have therefore included general information on our perfect dog - the Poodle.

Examples of cross-breeds

Bernadoodle: St Bernard and Standard Poodle

Cockapoo: Cocker Spaniel and usually Miniature Poodle

Maltipoo: Maltese and Toy or Miniature Poodle

Shizpoo: Shih Tzu and Toy or Miniature Poodle

A BRIEF HISTORY OF THE POODLE

Here is a dog breed that has been around for centuries. Through that time, it has been a military dog, a Hollywood pet, a circus dog, a pampered aristocratic and Royal companion, a hunter and fisherman's helper, a service dog and a family dog.

Poodles are classified as falling into the non-sporting group by the AKC, and he is one of the most popular breeds of dogs in both the US and the UK. He is majestic, fun, loyal, intelligent, and he has a long and fascinating history.

This is a great description of their general appearance from the AKC breed standard - "the Poodle has about him an air of distinction and dignity peculiar to himself" - but this doesn't mean that this beautiful dog is not fun-loving and a perfect companion. Far from it.

All Poodles are classed as one breed that comes in three recognized sizes, Standard, Miniature, and Toy (in the UK they fall into 3 separate breeds). All have been enjoying a boost in popularity in recent years. There is also a Medium Poodle, and even a Teacup, but these types are not always recognized as a breed in all countries.

The Standard Poodle is over 15 inches at the highest point of the shoulders. The Miniature Poodle is 15 inches or under at the highest point of the shoulders, with a minimum height above 10 inches. The Toy Poodle is 10 inches or under at the highest point of the shoulders.

Poodles are often considered aloof and aristocratic, but this could not be further from the truth.

They began life way back in medieval Germany when they were used as hunting retrievers or water dogs. This meant they often had to jump into lakes and rivers, hence the name 'Pudel' – it means 'to splash'. It is slightly controversial to state that they originated in Germany and not France, but I suspect Germany is closer to the mark! I also suspect that they were used to retrieve more than ducks.

But, wherever they began - probably before the 1200s, their love of water is why they have webbed feet and why their coat is the way it is. Their famous curly hair kept them warm and helped them to repel water. Even their clip had a purpose, and it is not new, as I will explain.

There is a picture painted in 1496 by Albrecht Dürer, and it is impossible not to recognize the clip shape that we see today. But it also points to the ancestry of the Poodle.

The dog seen in Albrecht Dürer paintings is thought to be a Portuguese Water Dog. One of the first descriptions of this dog is found in a monk's journal from 1297, where it is described as rescuing a dying sailor.

Portuguese Water Dogs were used by fishermen, not only as companions, but they helped herd the fish into nets.

The Portuguese Water Dog had what was called a lion clip, and it really does look like the coat of a lion. In the lion cut, the hindquarters, muzzle, and the base of the tail are shaved while the rest of the body is left full length. Sound familiar?

The lion cut lessened the shock of cold water when the dog jumped from the boat and provided warmth to the vital organs. The hindquarters were left shaved to allow more effortless movement of the back legs, and the tail acted as a rudder (and helped the fishermen to see them in the water). The Poodle clip that we see today is clear.

Although it has been adapted over the years, what is astonishing to see is that the fundamental, and unusual, cut, goes back much further than the French court or the circus' of England and France although the extravagance certainly emanated from there.

Poodles have been depicted in quite a few famous paintings. Even Rembrandt included one – his only full-length portrait - painted in 1631.

Despite all of this, Poodles are still most commonly associated with France, a country that fell in love with the Poodle in the mid-15th Century. Before the French Revolution, Louis XV was known to be very fond of poodles. Later, King Louis XVI and his wife Marie Antoinette were known for keeping smaller poodles at their palace in Versailles in the late 1700s.

In French, a Poodle is called a "Caniche" which roughly translates to "duck dogs" because they were used for hunting ducks. And it was in France that the Poodle that we know today was standardized. The French were so enamoured by their Poodle that it became the national dog breed of France – which might explain why you will have heard of the term French Poodle.

It was here, and during the reign of King Louis XVI, that the French began to trim Poodles in more outlandish styles and when they became fashionable with the aristocracy. It was also when the art of Poodle trimming emerged with the first professional canine stylists.

It was also around this time that our smaller sized-Poodles are said to have been introduced. Miniatures and Toys were bred as companion dogs and 'sleeve' dogs for Princesses and women of the court. Although bred to be smaller, it might have been a little later that we started to see the Miniature and Toy as recognized breeds.

During this time, the Standard Poodle remained a vital military dog – sniffing out explosives and hunting and guarding the enemy. Their intelligence, trainability, loyalty, and athleticism were perfect for this role.

So much so, that a black Poodle called Moustache became famous for serving in both the French Revolutionary and Napoleonic Wars in the early 1800s, fighting with Napoleon Bonaparte's army. He is a tremendous Poodle, both loyal and brave, who fought with his unit for well over 11 years, losing a leg and winning a medal along the way.

He was at many battles but in 1805, during the battle of Austerlitz, Moustache recovered the French flag from a fallen regimental standard bearer, losing a leg in the process. He was awarded a bravery medal which was engraved with the words "He lost his leg in the battle of Austerlitz and saved the colors of his regiment."

Moustache's reputation spread quickly, and orders were given that wherever he goes "he should be welcomed, en camarade; and thus he continued to follow the army. Having but three paws and one ear."

While our Standard Poodle was becoming well known as a military and war dog, our Toy and Miniatures – or our 'smaller' Poodles - were making a name for themselves, not just as dogs of the court and companions, but in the Circus.

Poodles are known for being one of the most intelligent of all dog breeds. Their athleticism and sociable nature added to a list of reasons that made them great Circus dogs in France and in England.

Poodles worked in the traveling circus', one of the few forms of entertainment available to the masses at the time. They were clipped to match the pom poms on the clown's outfits. It is thought that it was in the Circus that the styling really came to the fore, as Poodles were colored and had their hair styled to entertain.

It is also noted that it was in the French circus' of the 1800s, that the smaller sized Poodles started to become popular. This was for a good reason. The smaller dogs not only made great companions for life on the road, but the smaller size made it easier to travel.

Whatever the case, by the early 1800s as the breed size was becoming more differentiated, both Standard Poodles and the smaller Miniature and Toys took on the traditional cut. This 'unusual' clip appealed to cartoonists and artists who painted or drew Poodles in humorous poses. Examples include the caricature 'Monstrosities of 1821' featuring a Miniature Poodle and, in 1840, the famous Landseer satirical painting 'Laying Down the Law' that depicts a large Poodle. These artists made the Poodle's traditional clip famous.

By the mid- 1800s, breeders began importing Poodles to the USA, and in 1887 the AKA recognized the Poodle as a Standard Breed and classified it in the non-sporting group. I can't help feeling this should have been a controversial decision, given the history of the breed, particularly the Standard Poodle.

But by this time, they were already famous in England as show dogs – including the Miniatures. As they became famous for this, and as the shows became more competitive, the grooming of their coat became more extravagant.

After falling out of favor in the United States for a few years, in the 1930s, we saw the Poodles' popularity grow once more.

During the Great Depression of the 1920s, a small group of privileged men and women took an interest in purebred dogs.

One of these was Mrs. Byron Rogers of Misty Isles Kennels, who became known as the 'Poodle Revivalist". Her first Poodle, Anita von Luttersrpring, a German import, produced two champions in 1932 for Mrs. Shisman R. Hoyt. Both were black Poodles, and in those days, Poodles were mainly black or brown.

Mrs. Rogers also wrote for the AKC in its monthly Purebred Dogs Gazette before handing that mantle over to Mrs. Hoyt in around 1934. But her work, and that of Mrs. Hoyt, served to increase interest in this wonderful breed in the US.

By 1933, both German and English Poodles were creating a great deal of interest in the US, and this is when both Mrs. Rogers and Mrs. Hoyt traveled to Europe to visit kennels in England, France, and Switzerland. It was in England, that they went to the very first Poodle Speciality Show and when they first set eyes on a Poodle called Duc de la Terrace.

Mrs. Rogers wrote, "Duc de la Terrace is a superb large white, almost impossible to fault, and although he stands 25 inches at the shoulder, he is fine and beautifully proportioned. He has a perfect head, dark eyes and nose, wonderful feet, and the true wire coat so rare nowadays in Poodles. He deserves every win he has made!".

She didn't bring him home with her on that trip. But her parents heard her talk about this great dog and surprised their daughter with his purchase. They sent her to the docks, with a leash, to pick up an 'unusual' shipment.

She says of their first meeting, "He turned somewhat questioningly to us. 'It's all right, Duc, come along', and I laid my hands on his head. Gently he took my hand in his mouth, and so holding it went with us through the crowded New York streets until we found our car."

In August 1933, Nunse Duc de la Terrace of Blakeen had arrived in America. The same year that Miniature Poodles were recognized by the AKC, and the Toy Poodle was recognized in the Toy Group, (both in the non-sporting).

After entering and doing well in shows around the country, it was in 1935 that this famous Poodle won the Best in Show at the Westminster Kennel Club Dog Show.

It was this win that catapulted the breed into prominence. It really is a remarkable story, and if you ever get a chance, then the story of both dog and handler, Mrs. Hoyt, is a joy to read. This win also made her the first female handler to ever win the top prize.

There is no doubt that this win and the work done by these women helped build the love of Poodles around the country. As an aside, it was also arguably aided by the arrival of the electric trimmer. The new trimmer made the management of the Poodle's coat much easier for the average person.

The role of the Poodle as a military dog had not been forgotten however, and as the second world war loomed, the US Army started drafting Poodles as part of the 'Dogs For Defence' program. Once again, underlining their rise to prominence in the US and perhaps suggesting that they might not be 'non-sporting'.

Like the European Royalty that had gone before, the Hollywood royalty also loved their Poodles. Stars such as Audrey Hepburn, Bob Hope, Joan Collins, and Elvis Presley all had Poodles. There was even a Poodle skirt in the 1950s.

By 1961 the Poodle had become the most popular dog breed in the US, and it held the top spot until 1983. It has remained in the Top 10 ever since.

After centuries, these dogs were able to return to their hunting roots and are now competing in AKC retriever hunting tests and AKC Spaniel hunt tests.

They are excellent service dogs working as guide dogs for the blind, hearing dogs, and service dogs for mobility assistance.

But they remain one of the very best family dogs that anyone could hope to wish for.

THE POODLE CHARACTERISTICS

Poodles are great family dogs and exceptional companion dogs. They tend to have a long life - anything up to 14 years or more.

They are great with children, other pets and families although they are quite active with a tendency for hyper activity so they need a lot of exercise (other than Toy Poodles). Bear in mind that, as puppies, they can get over-excited and their bones are small (especially the Miniature and Toy Poodles). Coupled with their sensitivity to noise, this might mean they are not ideal for families with very young children.

Poodles are very easy to train, and due to their intelligence they do need trained, responding best to positive reinforcement.

They can your have fragile egos so you should never physically punish or use harsh words while training them. They can also go in a huff! Like elephants they can have a long memory and really don't like being scolded.

They can also be timid, and this can border on the neurotic. They can get easily stressed by noise and this might be caused by their hypersensitivity. But this also means that they can be highly attuned to our body language and to how we are feeling - they can be very empathetic and, of course they have strong loyalty tendencies. I suspect they assume this runs both ways!

Bear in mind that Poodles were once hunting dogs which means that they do need exercise and they do require training. They learn fast and if you do this early, which Poodles need, then you will have one of the best of dogs there is.

The smaller poodles can be protective which can make them aggressive to people or dogs outside of their immediate family, and they can easily develop bad habits such as nuisance barking, so you will want to ensure that they have early socialization and training to ensure that they get used to meeting new people and pets.

It should be remembered that poodles are basically hunting dogs in elegant attire, with a great deal of intelligence. They need exercise and training to be at their best.

Having said all of this, they love to play and they love attention, they will love you to the end of the world and back, and this makes them great fun and integral members of your household. Their personality is huge and in a few short weeks you won't be able to imagine a day, never mind your life, without them.

To keep them happy and their minds active you need to find games for you and your Poodle to play - and work out which games they love the most.

Early games such as hide-and-seek, run-around, find the ball, catch, and of course fetch and so on. These games are also great during training. Don't forget to switch up the games as they get older.

And, don't forget their Circus background too, so teach them tricks - roll-over, sit-up and get more adventurous. They will learn fast and unlike other hunting dogs like retrievers and spaniels, they like to solve a problem independently.

It pains me to say it, because the Poodle should be famous for so many things, but the coat of the Poodle is probably its most famous feature and they are most well-known for their curly, low-allergen coat.

Typically though, for this historic, individual, stubborn, loyal and fun-loving dog, a Poodle doesn't have fur like most dogs or animals. For most other beings, fur and hair grows to a certain point and then it must be shed.

Poodles are considered to have hair more like human hair but unlike human hair, Poodle hair grows only on a single, inner layer and, unlike fur or human hair, it does not shed. It will continue to grow unless there are hormonal changes or underlying issues and it won't fall out in large amounts.

This means you do need to trim and groom your Poodle regularly. But there is the added complication that the continuous growth means that rather than the fur coming off your dog, the longer hair gets tangled up in the surrounding hair and this is what leads to matting without proper care. And matting can be very painful.

In terms of the color of their coat, the standard was, for a long time black then white was added. Today Poodles come in all colors including back, white, grey, brown, apricot, silver, blue, cream.

The Parti Poodle refers to a mix of colouring, for example part white, part black/brown/red/blue and Parti Poodles can be found in all types of Poodles. They tend to be more expensive.

Poodles come in three sizes: the Standard, the Miniature and the Toy.

THE STANDARD POODLE

The Standard Poodle has a lifespan of 12-15 years and should be over 15 inches at the shoulder. They typically stand between 18–24 inches. The Female weight is anywhere between 40lbs and 50lbs and the male is anywhere between 60lbs - 70lbs but it can vary by a few pounds a the upper end of the scale.

They love advanced obedience competition that involve retrieving and jumping skills as well as agility competitions. Standard Poodles really benefit from mental stimulation and therefore, if you can take them along to advanced obedience classes.

Most Standard Poodles make great watchdogs and some even have mild (and sensible) protective instincts, but this is not an aggressive breed. Their attitude toward people varies from friendly to politely reserved. Early socialization is important to avoid excessive watchfulness or timidity.

Standard Poodles may also retain a strong prey drive and chase after birds or small animals. However, of all the Poodles, the Standard is the most laid-back.

THE MINIATURE POODLE

The Miniature should be between 10-15 inches and weigh
The Miniature Poodle has a lifespan of 13 to 15 years
Because he is smaller than the Standard he tends to be a more popular family dog or for those who live in apartments.

Like the other types of Poodle, Miniature Poodles are athletes and are easy to train. They too would benefit from advanced obedience and agility competitions.

Although this type of Poodle (like all both of the other types) should be 'square", meaning that their legs are long enough so that their height is more-or-less equal to their length, some Miniature Poodles can have shorter legs and a longer back. These dogs have inherited a physical deformity called chondrodysplasia and it might mean that they are more susceptible to disk disease (but square poodles can develop this, too).

THE TOY POODLE

Toy Poodles should be no more than 10 inches at the shoulder and weight 4lbs to 6lbs.

Like most small dogs they won't need as much exercise as either the Standard Poodle or the Miniature Poodle.

Also, like many small dogs, Toys are more likely than the other Poodles to have a tendency to bark too much if they are not well trained. It may because they can be more highly strung than the other types of Poodle.

The table below summarises the average hight and weight. The weight might vary by a pound or two at each end of the recommended scale.

	Standard	Miniature	Toy
Height	Over 15 inches at shoulders	10-15 inches at shoulders	No more than 10 inches
Weight	Female: 40-50 lbs Male: 60-70 lbs	10-15 lbs	4-6 lbs

All Poodles share a square outline, with a long, elegant neck and a straight back. They tend to have a leggy appearance with a long nose and dropped ears. You can't fail to notice their livery gait – the standard Poodles, especially, often move like a thoroughbred horse.

Other than size and weight there are some differences between our different Poodle breed types and we will cover these when, and if, they are relevant.

HEALTH, CARE AND WELLBEING

I n this chapter we cover the main areas of your Poodles general care as well as highlighting some of the most common health problem that your Poodle might experience at some point in his life. Don't worry too much because, overall, Poodles are healthy and don't have many, or any, major health issues.

The National Breed Club recommend the following tests:

- Hip Evaluation/Hip Dysplasia
- Ophthalmologist Evaluation
- Progressive Retinal Atrophy (PRA)
- Patella Evaluation

Additional :

- Von Willebrand Disease
- Osteochondrodysplasia (OCD)

Generally speaking Poodles are in good health. They will suffer from a range of minor problems, as most dogs do. Eye, knee, and hip tests are advised, as are DNA tests, which can identify PRA and von Willebrand's Disease.

ELBOW AND HIP DYSPLASIA

Poodles can be prone to hip and elbow dysplasia that usually progresses with age but it may start to be visible when still a puppy. It is an inherited disease, and is caused when the ball and sockets of the joint bones don't 'fit' properly and have a tendency to slip out. Screening of parent dogs is actively encouraged so that only dogs with sound joints are used for breeding.

It causes the joint to form abnormally which can cause not only pain but mobility problems. Early signs can be a wobbly walk or your puppy lying with splayed back legs (best described as looking like a frog). If your puppy does this it might be nothing to do with dysplasia but if you are worried you can ask your veterinarian to test his for the disease. There are a number of treatments including medication, physiotherapy and even surgery.

In the long term, that constant inflammation can lead to joint remodeling and premature arthritis. For some dogs, this can be disabling and impair their enjoyment of life, which is all the more heartbreaking because this can happen to young dogs.

Management of hip or elbow dysplasia means being careful of the puppy's activity levels whilst his bones are still maturing.

In addition, giving a joint supplement can help to protect the joint surfaces.

Dogs with mild dysplasia can often be managed with rest and pain-relieving medications, however, those most seriously affected may need surgery, including specialist replacement joint surgery.

The best way to ensure your dog is less prone to any of these conditions is to buy from a reputable breeder and to ensure you get health clearances from both of the parents.

LUXATING PATELLA

This is more common in Toy Poodles than Standard Poodles.

A Luxating Patella is fairly common in dogs and is is where the kneecap (patella) shifts sideways at the front of the knee. It can also be know as a dislocated kneecap.

The main symptom that is not often seen with other conditions is the sudden lifting of one hind limb. I have a dog with this condition. He lifts his leg for no apparent reason off the ground for a short time and continues to try and play. Some dogs will yelp when this happens while others, like my own dog, shows no signs of pain or discomfort. This is sometimes called a "skip" by both owners and vets.

Depending on the eternity of the condition rest or complete rest might be recommended. If it is severe then there is an operation that can might help but as with any surgery, that too, comes with risks and complications.

OSTEOHONDRODYSPLASIA

Osteochondrodysplasia is a is a disorder ("dysplasia") of bones ("osteo") and cartilage ("chondro"). It is an inherited is what is know as an Autosomal Recessive manner. It means that it needs a mutated gene from each parent.

It was discovered in the Miniature Poodle in Britain in 1956 when it was first described a crippling dwarfism. It is a form of skeletal dysplasia that stunts growth and impairs movement and it can be seen when a pup is only 3 weeks old. Affected pups soon exhibit abducted hind limbs, enlarged joints, flattening of the rib cage, shortened and bent long bones, undershot jaws, and elongated and misshapen paws that resemble clubfoot.

Affected dogs can survive for many years with supportive care and they will develop arthritis and might have breathing difficulty due to their deformed ribcages.

It is not known how rare or common this is but it can be tested for and is one of the reason you need to ensure that you know the test for both of your puppy's parents. This is important if you intend your puppy to have a litter because a dog can be a carrier without any symptoms.

GASTRIC DILATATION VOLVULUS (GDV) OR BLOAT

Poodle's can be prone to something called Gastric Dilatation Volvulus (GDV). This is when the stomach fills with air and twists on its axis preventing the passage of food and water which can stop the flow of circulation to the stomach and intestines. This can be life-threatening.

It is a serious condition and as soon as this happens you must take your dog to the vet right away. If the stomach is not returned to its natural position then it can be fatal.

To prevent this happening, try not to feed him for at least 30-45 minutes before exercise and don't feed him until as least 30-45 minutes after exercise. You can also reduce the chances of bloat by feeding small meals spread throughout the day and by using a bowl designed to make it difficult for your dog to eat too quickly.

EARS AND SKIN

The Poodle grows hair inside their ears and therefore you should clean their ears regularly to prevent earwax from accumulating and to reduce the chance of infection.

If you notice a smell, or you notice black or brown wax, or his ear looks red and he is scratching it then he may have an ear infection.

Otitis Externa is one of the most common conditions amongst many dog breeds but is more likely to affect Cocker Spaniels, Poodles, Bassets and GSD's. You will notice a wax build-up or a smell and probably both.

Otitis is also often one of the illnesses that insurance companies exclude from policies as an on-going condition so check this out before you enrol. This is probably due to the fact that, once susceptible, it is likely to keep recurring.

Regularly cleaning your Poodles's ears can make all the difference to preventing Otitis taking hold but do not over-clean as this can actually make it worse.

To help avoid this as much as possible you will need to check and clean your Poodle's ears regularly. Ask your veterinarian about appropriate ear care products then gently wipe out the ear with a cotton ball moistened with the cleaning solution that has been recommended. Avoid sticking the cotton swabs into his ear canal because that could damage it . If you are worried about how to clean his ears, then just ask your veterinarian to show you how best to clean them. I know that I have done that in the past.

To get him used to having his ears touched make sure you remember to touch and caress them when he is a puppy.

Like the ears, allergies can cause problems with the skin and they can lead to *dermatitis* (skin inflammation). They can be caused by many things including pollen or dust mites, items your dog eats (for example, wheat), items that your dog comes into contact with (for example, washing powders), or bites from parasites such as fleas.

As allergies cannot be cured, treatment might be needed for the rest of his life. But it is usually very effective and won't impact him other than requiring regular mediation. You will be provided with special shampoo and sometimes steroids. I try to avoid steroids for long term use if I can but they can be effective in the short-term. There are quite a few medications on the market that your vet might recommend and I have used many of them.

I ended up back at steroids but managed to significantly reduce the requirement by switching to hypoallergenic dog food. It took about 4-6 weeks to really see the benefit but it worked incredibly well.

Coconut oil may be used as a treatment for parasites, but it is recommended to consult with your vet first. Coconut oil has been proven over the years to contain both antimicrobial and antibacterial properties. Apply a small amount of this to your Poodle's ear canal and it may help prevent ear mites and yeast infection. Again, I have tried this and it helped a little but it didn't solve the problem.

You may want to consider feeding your Poodle less starchy meats and food. Starch is known to slow down metabolism, which in turn may affect its inflammatory response. Cut chicken and whole grain foods from his diet and substitute them with more turkey or beef.

Sebaceous Adenitis

Sebaceous adenitis is a rare inflammatory skin disease that affects the skin glands of young and middle age dogs. It tends to effect the Standard Poodle but all Poodles should be tested.

Symptoms include Alopecia, mild scaling of skin along the head, trunk and ears and there might be a secondary bacterial infection along the hairline (more common in long haired breeds).

The cause is still unknown and if your dog is diagnosed with this then you might want to be included in a tracking survey so that more can be found out about this disease.

EYES

Progressive retinal atrophy (PRA)

PRA this tends to effect the Miniature Poodle are than the other type of Poodle and is a part of the test that your breeder will carry out.

The retina is part of the central nervous system. In retinal degeneration, the cells of the retina stop working leading to impaired vision and blindness. There are lots of causes for retinal degeneration including other eye conditions, diet, reactions to other drugs, genetics.

It is a group of disease that worsens over time and, according to PetMD, there is no effective cure. Because diet can cause retinal degeneration, providing your dog with a balanced (that includes meat), low-fat diet might help improve or slow the degeneration.

Glaucoma

Also ask your breeder if the Poodles parents have been recently screened for Glaucoma. Poodles suffer from Glaucoma (Toy Poodles appear to be most prone to this). Symptoms include squinting, watery eyes, bluing of the cornea, and redness in the whites of the eyes and it is very painful.

Eyelash disorders

Trichiasis, distichiasis, and ectopic cilia are eyelash conditions that are more common in Miniature and Toy Poodles and some other dog breeds.

Whether causes by an in-growing eyelash (Trichiasis) or ones that grow from inside the eyelid (ectopic cilia) all of them can damage the cornea of the eye and can also cause conjunctivitis. In all cases you will notice and overflow of tears.

TEETH

You will start getting your puppy used to having something in his mouth at an early age so that he will be comfortable with you cleaning his teeth when he gets older and needs it.

Use a dog tooth brush or, if you don't have one, then you can use a child's toothbrush. You should clean his teeth at last twice a week, and ideally every day. You can also use a dog dental chew. They love these, just don't overdo it - remember they are not treats.

NAILS

Trim his nails once or twice a month. If you tend to walk on hard surfaces his nails will get worn down naturally and you may only need to get his nails checked or cut when he goes to the groomer. If you can hear them clicking on the floor, they might be too long.

Dog toenails have blood vessels in them, and if you cut too far you can cause bleeding so you might want to start by watching a groomer or asking for help from your veterinarian.

COAT AND GROOMING

Poodles are a good choice for allergy sufferers, because, as we already know, they don't shed like other breeds.

However, the poodles dense, curly coats need groomed and trimmed every 4-6 weeks. And you need to factor this into the cost of their care.

The range of cuts and clips available for Poodles is vast and Poodle grooming requires a book in itself.

Rather than exploring all of the cuts and clips we will cover the basics of grooming.

Most owners have their poodle's coat cut to one short length, in a style known as the sporting clip and the show clips of poodles require many hours of brushing and care.

Poodles who are left with their manes to grow need daily brushing to avoid their curly coats becoming matted. If this happens the only option is to shave them down.

The texture of the coats ranges from soft and wavy to coarse and curly.

When you are grooming him, don't forget to check for any signs of infection such as redness, tenderness, or inflammation on the skin, eyes, and on his feet. This means that your weekly groom will help you spot any potential health problems early.

DEW CLAWS

The first thing to point out is that dogs very rarely have dew claws in their hind legs - they are almost always only seen in the front legs - just above their pad and below the carpal pad. I tend to think about it as a thumb because it really is a thumb. While you can expect your Poodle to have two dewclaws, this is not the case for all breeds. The Great Pyrenees, for example, should have six dewclaws, one on each front leg and two on each hind leg and this is an AKC requirement.

When I was young, dew claws were removed from puppies when they were very young (anywhere between two and five days old) to 'conform to the breed standard'. It was also said that the dew claw might tear in later life and this would be very painful (it is). In those days, tails were docked at the same time depending on the breed requirements. I had the experience of being present during this process for all five of our first litter and it was not a pleasant experience. When dew claws are removed, the toe is severed off at the joint so that the entire toe is removed. It was, and still is, done without anaesthesia using an instrument that can only be described as a plier.

The practice of automatically removing dew claws in very young puppies is not as common these days. I no longer believe that they should be removed, and in later litters that I raised, we neither removed the dewclaws nor docked their tails. To this day I have never had a problem with one of my dogs' dew claws and have only recently known of a dog, a Cockapoo, who had a problem with his dew claw (he is 3 years old). Even although he had torn his dew claw while out running, the vet opted to fix the dew claw and not remove it. So, why did the vet simply cut the nail back and not remove the dew claw?

One of the reasons is that dew claws are attached to other tendons and muscles. The front dew claws contain two bones. Attached to these bones are four tendons and two muscles. Once the dew claw is removed, these muscles are then left to atrophy, weakening the entire structure of the carpus and this can cause arthritis in the carpal.

The dew claws function is to stabilize the carpal joint when the dog is running or when he is making sharp turns. This stabilizing action gives additional traction and reduces the tension on the front leg. If a dog does not have its front dew claws, the leg will twist on its axis to overcompensate. This increases the pressure on the carpus and in turn, the rest of the forelimb all the way up to the shoulder.

A study published by the Journal of the American Veterinary Medical Association in 2018 looked at the risk factors for injuries in dogs involved with agility events. They concluded that the absence of the front dewclaws was one of the greatest factors "associated with significantly increased odds of injury". They went as far as to advise against the removal of the front dew claws from dogs being used in agility type activities.

The argument to remove the dew claw 'incase of future injury' is, I believe, outweighed by the other, more serious and longer lasting injuries that we now know can be caused if a dog does not have its dew claw to help reduce the strain on other parts of his leg.

LOSS OF BLOOD/WEIGHT

One of the first questions you should get asked by a veterinarian if you need to make an emergency call because your dog has had an injury is "is your dog bleeding". The reason they ask this is not because a dog can lose a lot of blood but that, even a small loss of blood, can be dangerous. Just two teaspoons per pound of weight can be enough to put your dog into shock. It is for this reason, if nothing else, that it is useful to always know the weight of your dog.

Von Willebrand Disease - this is a blood clotting disorder frequently found in Toy and Miniature Poodles. Ask your breeder for the test - this is a DNA test.

EATING POOP

It is not uncommon for a puppy to eat his poop - around 25% of them do it. Sometimes it is something they copied from watching their mother. When puppies are very young, and before they are weaned a mother eats her puppy's poop. This can continue during the early part of weaning. For us humans, it's quite hard to watch but it's perfectly natural for dogs. It is thought that it dates back to the days when they lived in the wild when the mother would need to keep the den clean and free from poop to protect the den from predators (and infections). For some puppies they will watch and learn this behavior but it usually doesn't last long.

Sometimes it's simply because puppies love taste and textures, and poop has both of these, plus it carries lots of interesting scents that has lots of information. Who the owner might be, what did they eat? And don't forget, puppies only have their mouths to explore with.

Research has found that dogs most likely to eat poop are hungry. If he is continuing to eat poop then make sure that you are feeding his at the correct intervals, and in the correct amounts and preferably to a schedule. You might also want to check that the food contains enough of the ingredients that he needs.

They can also eat poop because they are bored or stressed. Make sure he is not being left alone for too long and is getting plenty of stimulation. If you need to work, and are out of the house, try and get a dog sitter to visit.

Of all the reasons your puppy is eating poop the least likely is a nutritional deficiency in his diet. If he suddenly starts eating poop, especially if he is a bit older, then it might be due to a medical problem and in this instance you should contact your veterinarian.

TO SPAY OR TO NEUTER YOUR DOG ?

Every dog owner is going to come up against this question but there really isn't any definitive right or wrong answer, either on the best timing or whether it needs to be done at all.

In the USA vets tend to recommend that pups are neutered or spayed as early as possible, usually around 8 weeks. In Europe and the UK most vets recommend 6–9 months and some recommend waiting until 10-24 months for males while females should be allowed to have at least two seasons.

It is now generally recommended that your dog has reached maturity before being spayed or neutered. This is because neutering and spaying removes hormones from your dog which have an important role to play in their development. These hormones regulate growth, mood, muscle, bone growth and density.

Some studies have shown an increased rate of, for example, Hip Dysplasia, in dogs that have been neutered before maturity. If there is no medical reason to do it early, waiting until your dog reaches maturity might be better.

For female dogs, there are the added questions around whether it is beneficial to let the dog have a season before it is spayed. There is no evidence to show that having a season is in any way a healthy option for the dog, but the arguments about leaving a dog to reach maturity stand.

These are just some details of the pro's and con's but you should always check with your veterinarian.

SPAYING

Spaying is the removal of the reproductive organs of the female dog and it can be either the removal of the uterus and ovaries or just the ovaries (which can be done using keyhole surgery). Removing both the uterus and the ovaries involves an abdominal operation and this is a bigger operation that requires an incision and needs a longer recovery time. It tends to be the most common operation. Regardless of the method the pro's and con's are the same.

The most obvious reason for spaying your dog is to avoid unwanted pregnancies closely followed by avoiding the regular seasons when he will be in heat. The medical benefits include reducing the risk of cancer in his reproductive organs and reducing the risk of Pyometra (which affects 23% of female dogs and leads to cysts in his uterus) and a reduced risk of perianal fistula (this is also known as anal furunculosis and more commonly affects German Shepherd Dogs). If it is done before he is 2.5 years old it can also reduce the risk of cancer in his mammaries .

Some of the arguments against spaying include the increased risk of urinary incontinence and increased urinary tract infections. It can also increase the risk of an under-active thyroid and increase the risk of obesity. If the dogs are spayed before puberty there is a higher risk of vaginitis, and if done before 12 months (this timing will depend on the size of your dog) it can increase the risk of bone cancer.

NEUTERING

The operation for neutering your male dog is not as big as the female abdominal spay, The operation involves the removal of both testicles. After the operations it might look as if the dog still has his testes because the scrotal sac might initially retain the normal shape. It will usually shrink down over time.

One of the main reasons for neutering will be the desire to reduce the risk of your dog roaming in search of a female in season. We had a dog that did this and it was incredibly stressful. It made me think long and hard about what to do with Barney (he hasn't be spayed). The medical arguments for neutering include reducing the risks of testicular cancer and non cancerous prostate problems as well as reducing the risk of perineal fistula (again, more common with German Shepherd Dogs than Poodles).

The main arguments for not neutering include increasing the risk of hypothyroidism and obesity, and increasing the risk of prostate cancer. If it is done before he is 1 year of age there is an increased risk of bone cancer

For both sexes, the argument against neutering is the increased risk of an adverse reaction to vaccinations.

Finally, neutering will not fix behavioral problems including things like aggression and disobedience or resource guarding.

OVERHEATING

High internal temperatures can be a serious health issue for all dogs as well as Poodles. It can lead to organ failure and even death. Dog's don't sweat - they can only do so via their paws and they cool themselves by panting.

A dog's internal temperature is normally around 100 to 102.5, and a temperature of 105 or above is considered to be a crisis.

The most common culprit of critical overheating is the car. Cars can heat up very, very fast. A car parked in the sun can reach a temperature of 116 within 60 minutes. The interior, such as the dashboard, can even reach over 150 degrees Farenheit.

- Cracking a window won't help much - but if you have a sunroof or moon roof then leave that open at all times. Heat rises and so this will help but it won't remove the problem.

If you already know about the car then you now need to think about your walk and exercise - especially if it there are high temperatures and high humidity.

- Try to avoid walking your dog on hot pavements especially asphalt. Black asphalt not only retains heat but it radiates heat. Your dog will be much closer to this heat than you are.

- If you dog has been playing he might not think about having a drink. Make sure he has a good drink before your walk and afterwards.

- If your dog is panting heavily and his tongue is hanging out and you notice he is more lethargic or slower than normal then your dog might be overheating. You need to get him out of the sun and cool him down right away.

- One of the best ways to cool him down is to get him into cool water. The best heat transfer points are paws, groin, and cheeks so if for any reason you can't get him into a bath or a natural water source then put cool water over these areas first - along with his tummy.

- Shaving off all of his coat is not believed to work very well (and can actually aide the heating process because his coat actually protects him from the heat too) but shaving his tummy can be a good idea and helps you cover his groin area faster.

PLANNING AHEAD

Before you bring your puppy to his forever home, you need to find out what type of food your puppy has been eating up until this point. Your breeder will be happy to let you know and should provide you with a starter pack of what they have been feeding his. Don't worry if they don't do this as standard practice, just make sure that you know what you need to have in the house for the arrival of your new puppy.

You will introduce him to the food you want to use slowly by mixing some of his existing food into the new food that you have chosen. Slowly increase the proportion of his new food over a period of 7-1o days. You also need to know how often he was being fed, and at what time because, initially, you will stick to this pattern and gradually change it if you need to do so.

You do this because any sudden change to his diet will upset his tummy. It will make him feel uncomfortable and can result in unexpected accidents caused by diarrhoea which your puppy won't be able to control. It simply makes it more difficult to successfully start potty training in these first few important days.

As you start to slowly change over his food you can also start to gradually change the time at which he gets his food so that the schedule moves to the times that works within your household.

If you need to change his food at any point in his life then you will always repeat the process of gradually mixing in the old food with the new. Dogs - and their stomachs - don't like a sudden change to their diet so always remember to introduce a new dog food slowly, no matter how old he is.

In order to get help him settle quickly in his new home you will need to make sure that you have something that smells familiar to him when he arrives. If the breeder doesn't have something you can take home with you, then ask if you can leave some clothing for him for a at least a week so that you can take it home with your puppy (a sock or an old towel will do).

Once he arrives home, put this item into the crate or basket that you want his to use. This will give your puppy some comfort over the first few days, and be a familiar smell which should help him settle in.

Finally, if you have a yard or garden, you will need to puppy-proof it. If there are any gaps in a fence or hedge, your puppy will find it, and he will disappear in a second to go exploring. You can use plastic chicken-wire or something similar but anything that will securely block access will do.

Don't forget that your puppy will want to chew things inside the home too, so you will need to puppy-proof any electrical wires (move them out of reach if you can) along with house-plants, some of which are poisonous to him.

You will want all of the family involved in his early training and you need to think about this before he arrives. Work out who can do what and try and get all your household members on board as early as you can (this is also good for helping to prevent separation anxiety). You might want to try and get agreement on who does the morning, or lunch or evening care or who's job it is to think up a game to play on a particular day.

And don't forget to pick the name of your puppy!

HOW TO CHOOSE A NAME

Your puppy might already have a name, but if you are reading this before you have picked your puppy's name, then here are a few tips which can help you decide. A good name can even make training easier.

Dogs hear at a higher frequency range than we do, and so choosing a name that ends with a vowel sound will help to grab his attention.

Names that end in an 'ie ar 'ay' sound are best. Ideally, the name should start with a hard letter sound like B or D, and ideally, it should contain two syllables. For example Millie, Poppy, Barney, Paddy or even Tootsie.

But remember, you want to avoid any names that your puppy might confuse with one of your cues (like sit, stay, down, here or come).

Try and say the name a few times too because you need to make sure all the members of your family can say it - especially if they are toddlers - and that everyone is comfortable to shout the name in the park.

Although it's better to use his name from the very start, don't worry if you take a day or two to find just the right name that seems to fit your puppy's personality as you get to know him over these first few days.

If you have a dog from a shelter, and you really want to change his name, or don't know what his name used to be, then give him a few days to get used to it (but it might take him a bit longer).

To him get to know his name you need to help him along. When you say it, reward him at the same time even if there is no response. Then, as soon as there is a response, for example he looks in your direction, immediately reward him with a tastier treat and lots of praise. In the beginning he will be responding to the sound of your voice rather than to his name but he will soon put two and two together.

Walk around the house and say his name and reward his response. Getting your puppy used to his name can be fun for all of us.

WELCOME HOME

W hen your pup comes home, you will ideally already have his crate or basket ready. You will have the same type of dog food that he was being fed, and you will have the item placed in his crate or basket that smells familiar to his from his previous home.

Over the first few nights, he is likely to miss his old family. It is okay, over the first nights, to take his crate or basket into your room, but only do this for the first few nights.

He also won't be used to lots of noise and activity around him. Try and keep things as calm as possible, and make sure to remember to allow him some 'time-outs'.

To introduce him to his crate, place it in the room that you tend to spend most of your time. If you have a room you want your puppy to stay in, then, after a day or two, move the crate into this room - but make sure you and the rest of the family spend time with him in that room.

And don't forget that puppies sleep a lot and they need their sleep. They will easily sleep for 7-8 hours at night, and they can sleep up to 14 hours a day. I will talk about a schedule later.

But, in the early days, try to make sure that he gets his sleep time. Everyone will want to play with him. This is okay, and it's good for your puppy to have lots of affection and attention because it will help him to get familiar with people and being handled, but try and ensure that he gets a little break to get some sleep.

In terms of picking him up and cuddling him, try not to overdo his handling. Constantly picking him up will be something his little body is unlikely to be used to. Just like us, if we get picked up too much, it can become uncomfortable and even painful.

This isn't anything to worry about, but it's useful to be aware of how often he is being handled.

The best way to pick up your young puppy is to put your hands around his chest, then pull him towards your chest. As soon as he is safely secured, take one of your hands and use it to support his bottom so that you are supporting his weight - much like a baby.

Finally, don't forget to take a sniff of his breath. A puppy's breath has a unique smell, so grab your chance while you can. It disappears quickly!

VACCINATIONS OVER THE FIRST YEAR

It's a good idea to talk to your vet about your puppy's vaccination requirements as soon as you can. Below is a summary of the recommended vaccinations from the American Kennel Club. There are some other vaccinations so talk to your local veterinary about any requirements in your area.

Recommended vaccinations:

- 6-8 weeks - Distemper, parvovirus
- 10-12 weeks - DHPP (for distemper, adenovirus (hepatitis), parainfluenza, parvovirus
- 16-18 weeks DHPP, rabies

- 12-16 months DHPP, rabies

Unvaccinated puppies less than 4 months old are most at risk of Parvovirus. This is contagious and affects all dogs and there is no cure and is one of the main reason that you don't want your unvaccinated puppy to meet any dogs that you don't know.

You can take him to your yard around 7 days after his first set of vaccinations, but still avoid other dogs especially if you don't know them. Your yard must be enclosed to ensure no other dogs have been there. Don't let his feet touch the ground in public spaces.

If you live in an apartment, you might need to go outside to a public or well-used street during his potty training so that he can relieve himself. Pick one spot, and carry him there and back but you can let him sniff around that spot.

After his second vaccination, you can take him for a walk on paved surfaces, but not on grass or places where you can't see if other dogs have urinated or gone to the toilet.

It is still important for his not to meet unfamiliar dogs.

The Kennel Club recommends talking to your veterinarian about heartworm treatment when your puppy is 12-16 weeks old. This is a preventative medication that is taken regularly.

These are the sort of issues where any recommendation must come from a qualified pet health professional who understands the laws, and problems in your area, and who will be aware of any breed-specific problems. Make sure that you ask your veterinarian for advice.

Your puppy can go outside for a walk in the park after his third set of vaccinations (around weeks 16-18). It is also at this point that he can exercise for up to 20 minutes at a time.

Finally, he can meet unfamiliar dogs. At this stage, when he is around 18 weeks, you can also take him to his puppy socialization classes at the local pet store or your vet (and where all the puppies will be at the same vaccination stage).

SOCIALIZATION

In its simplest form, socialization is how you and your puppy learn to communicate with each other and how your puppy learns about those that he lives with or meets. It is how he learns to live in 'society' and how to interact with thing he meets including humans and other dogs.

Having as many happy encounters as possible during his early weeks helps his to relate appropriately to humans of all ages, other dogs and to situations that he will face day-to-day throughout his life.

This isn't easy in the first week or two because your puppy has yet to be vaccinated.

However, you can still carry him, take him out in your car, and have friends and family come to the house to meet him. Try and let him meet as many adults and children as you can in the weeks before you can take him to classes. He should also meet other dogs at home if you know them, and you know that they are fully vaccinated.

This is also the best time to touch his ears, mouth, tails, and paws and to get his used to you doing this. This part of puppy training is often missed, but it will really help later with grooming, or if you need to inspect him for an injury or when he goes to the vet for an examination.

Sit with him quietly so that you are also teaching him how to relax with you, and touch his ears or mouth, run your hand over his paws and his tail, and give him a treat and reward when he remains calm and relaxed.

If you can, and as soon as you are allowed - and after his

vaccinations allow it - take your puppy to socialization classes so that he can meet other young puppies and their parents.

They will play around for 20 or 30 minutes, but they learn how to communicate with dogs that they don't know and they will learn how 'far they can go'. Dogs are pretty good at letting each other know when enough-is-enough! They also learn about meeting new humans who are not part of the family.

This part of his early training helps him feel comfortable with dogs he doesn't know and he will learn what he can and can't do without getting a bark or, occasionally a nip, and he will be learning about meeting and interacting with humans.

HOUSE AND POTTY TRAINING

One of the main reasons people don't want to have a puppy is the thought of potty training, or specifically, the thought of a dog that is not house-trained and that messes in the home.

House training or potty training your puppy will be one of the first things you do when your puppy comes home. It can be done, so don't worry. In fact, in the years to come you will forget that you ever had to house-train your beloved dog and won't even remember how you did it.

The speed at which a puppy learns will vary from puppy to puppy. How fast he learns can be helped by any training that had started in his previous home. I know this sounds obvious, but even a young puppy's rate of being house trained will depend on what they were taught once they were weaned.

When we had a litter of 7 spaniels and we started to train the puppies to go to the puppy pad as soon as they reached the stage of moving around (this is around the time they are being weaned) and as they moved on to solid food. It meant that when it was time to go to their forever homes they were much easier to potty train.

They were also familiar with using a cage. We kept it in the room with them so that they could wander in to play and sleep (and get used to its sound). It really can help a great deal.

HOW LONG CAN A PUPPY WAIT FOR THE TOILET

Don't forget that a puppy's bladder grows with them. So when they are younger, it is smaller, which means that they will need to empty it more often.

Generally speaking, a puppy's ability to hold its bladder increases by about an hour per month.

This will mean that at one month, they can hold on for about an hour. By 2 months old, they should be able to hold on for about 2 hours before they need to relieve themselves.

Try not to make them hold on for much more than this over the first few months or there will be accidents. And aim to make sure that your time away from them can tie into their need to go to the toilet.

As a general rule, puppies under 6 months will struggle to hold their bladder for more than 3 or 4 hours, and this should help you work out how long you can be away or when you might need to try and get someone to visit your puppy so that they can relieve themselves outside, rather than in their crate, or in the room they are in.

In terms of pooping, a puppy will poop after food. If you feed your puppy before you leave, make sure that you feed them around 45 minutes before you are due to leave.

This gives you time to take them for a poop. They will normally need to poop between 5 and 30 minutes after a meal.

If you are playing with your puppy before you leave, take them out for a poop after the playtime, as this can also make them want to poop.

Puppy pads should not replace taking your puppy outside often and encouraging him to toilet. Take him out often and praise him every time he toilets.

PUPPY PADS

The best thing I have used for potty training is puppy pads, and the very best thing I ever tried, was a puppy pad that looked like grass. For some reason, it really works. I used it with the seven puppies before they left for their forever homes, and they all used it. They would actually go to it without any prompting.

Whether you use a fabric pad or a fake grass one, these are the things you need to do.

Place the puppy pad in the room that he is going to be in. Start doing this the day he comes home. The he looks like he is about to potty, put him on the pad. If he relieves himself, give him lots of praise.

You will soon work out what his behavior is when he needs to toilet so keep an eye on him so that you can react each time. It won't take long - probably around 2-3 days - before he will go to the pad.

Once he is regularly using the pad, start moving it towards the door that you want him to use to go out. Try not to move it too far from where you started the training; just move it slowly to that door.

Once at the door, let him get used to that for a day or two before moving the pad just outside it.

In the final stages, if you notice him starting to toilet in the house, gently pick him up and place him on an 'emergency' pad. Then take him and the pad outside. If there is not enough time to do this, just place him on the pad.

You might want to consider placing the puppy pad at the door that he will be using to access his outside area right away. Of course, this will depend on how far away from the room the household congregates is from that door. You don't want to place it too far from where he will be spending most of his time in these early days.

At every point, every little win, give your puppy lots of praise.

This process can take more time for some puppy's than for others. However, as long as you remember that he will want to relieve himself when he wakes up, after play, and after he eats, then you have a head-start knowing when to expect activity. Make sure you take him outside after each of these events - *don't only rely on the puppy pad.*

It's important never to punish or get angry with your puppy if he toilets in the house. You sometimes see a recommendation to push their face into the mess. Don't do this. It will do the opposite of helping. They won't understand and will be scared. Particularly your Poodle. Getting angry or pushing them may only mean that they don't want to potty in front of you and learn to avoid it as well as making them feel anxious around you.

HOW TO MANAGE THEIR POTTY TRAINING

Puppy's (and later dogs) love praise and rewards.

Once your puppy begins the process of going outside to potty, don't forget that every time he relieves himself outdoors, you need to praise his and give him a treat.

Don't do this while he is in the action of potty-time - he will stop to seek the reward, get distracted, and won't finish what he started. It means that he won't be fully relieved when he goes back inside. Instead, wait until he has finished, and don't forget to do this every single time he goes outdoors to potty.

As you do this, use a phrase that he will start to recognize (try not to use 'Good boy' or 'Good girl' - it might cause confusion!).

Instead, use a short phrase such as 'potty' or 'pee pee' or whatever you feel comfortable saying and will remember - just make sure it is one that your pup can begin to recognize with the action he is being asked to complete. This is a key step because they need to know exactly what behavior the reward is for.

This is not only useful when your puppy is young. Millie, my older dog, had soft tissue damage to his knee on his hind leg. This meant that he struggled to walk and had difficulty 'sitting down' to toilet.

When I carried her to the garden to try and get her to 'do pee-pee,' this was much easier because I could say a phrase, and she knew exactly what I wanted her to do.

It's good to remember that much of what you teach your puppy now will be of great help throughout your his life. It's also good to think about what phrase you will be stuck with for a long time!

In his early days you will be tempted to take him into the yard every hour to play with him - try not to overdo the this. Stick to around 15 minutes at a time. And don't confuse him by taking him out to play when you want him to potty.

I had someone do this with their puppy and they couldn't understand why he did not potty outside. The problem was that the puppy thought outside was only for play and didn't know what was expected of him. The puppy had lots and lots of fun but his mum was getting more and more frustrated. Try and set a clear distinction between when you are taking him out to potty and when you are taking him out to play. The schedule will help plan this and help train you to do both potty and play.

If you live in a flat that has two access doors, then use one for play and one for potty!

Where?

Choose a place or a small area outside that you want him to use to relieve himself. As he relieves hisself, say your word or specific phrase.

Always take him to the same place every time you take him out to potty - in the morning, the last thing at night, after food, or after play.

If you are using training pads overnight, take the soiled pad to the outside area where you want your puppy to toilet. The scent can help him.

When it is time to take him outside to toilet, avoid playing with him and getting him excited before he relieves himself. Remember, he is easily distracted and will forget what he is there to do.

If your puppy looks a bit confused or doesn't toilet right away, try to encourage him to sniff the ground beside the area you want him to use.

Stay outside until he toilettes. If nothing happens after 5 minutes, don't start to play with him but take his back inside and watch him closely.

After 10 minutes, take him out again and repeat the process until he has done what you need him to do.

THE SIGNS TO WATCH OUT FOR

Try and supervise your puppy at all times when you are trying to potty train him. I know this is very hard to do, but by supervising and watching him, you will notice how he looks when he starts to feel uncomfortable because his bladder is full, and you will start to recognize how he reacts when this happens.

For example, he might start circling or sniffing the floor, he might be restless, and he may try and go to a place where he has previously done his business.

If you see your puppy mid-toilet, pick him up and take him outside and try to get him to finish what he started; if he does, then gently praise him.

Now, this is hard to describe, and it's not something that is often said, but watch your puppy's bottom.

When they need to go poop, you will notice their anus swelling outwards. This means a poop is imminent. To this day, I watch my dogs rear ends when we are out walking (usually it's the start of a walk), and I get the poop bags ready.

As you will have learned already, puppies and dogs are all different in how they prefer to poop and pee.

When Millie was a puppy, she was obviously getting restless and looking around for a place to go but when Barney was young, he was really difficult to read because he didn't do any obvious things like scratching at the door, sniffing, or circling. He just 'looked a certain way' and was restless in a different way that he usually was.

Watch out for any of those signs, or watch out for something your dog does that might signal a change in behavior. This is the part where they train us. We need to watch and learn what they are telling us.

I would, though, also recommend keeping them to just one or two rooms as you go through the house-training process—be vigilant; watch, learn, and stay with them if you can,

LEAVING THE HOUSE AND OVERNIGHT

It is possible that your puppy won't be able to hold his bladder all night long for several months. This means that he will need to relieve himself during the night.

Put some newspaper or puppy pads in his crate. Try and place them in an area that he can avoid. In the morning, don't forget to remove the soiled pad or newspaper and then take it to his outside area to try and draw him to the scent.

If you are going out for any length of time, and you are using his crate, then you will do the same thing. If you can, don't be away for more than 2-3 hours at the start.

It may take several months before your puppy is fully house trained, but the accidents will become less frequent. Try and be patient. It will pay off in time, and in just a few short years, you will have forgotten all about the trials and tribulations of potty training your puppy.

HOW TO CLEAN UP

It's important to clean the area and try to remove the scent.

Don't use ammonia-based products as this will just encourage them to go to the same place again. I have found that cold water can do the trick too (and it is very good at removing any staining). You can use biological powder, and some people swear by a vinegar-water mix. I have tried this, but I am not convinced it works, although I know of other dog owners for whom it has worked wonders.

YOUR SCHEDULE

One of the best and most effective ways to train your puppy is to get him used to a schedule.

When you first bring your puppy home, make sure that you take him out frequently. Take him out as soon as he wakes up, after playing, and after he has eaten or had a drink.

4 step summary of a puppy schedule:-

1. Feed them at the same time and the same frequency, for example, every 2 hours depending on their age

2. Take them out them out as soon as they wake up
3. Take them out before they go to bed
4. Take them out after food and after indoor puppy play.

In terms of how a day might look, try not to forget his sleep time. Your puppy will get sleepy after eating but make sure that you take him out to potty before he goes for his nap.

I tend to let my dogs out as soon as they wake up. I then feed them breakfast and play with them for 20-30 minutes (depending on how much time I have), then I take them out again before they fall asleep.

They have been doing this schedule since they were young pups, and they seem to like it. These days, as adults, Barney will potty as soon as he wakes up but Millie is more interested in breakfast and so will wait until after she has been fed. They will both urinate as soon as they wake up and before breakfast.

Finally, once he is older don't feed him right before you take him out for a walk and don't feed him as soon as you return from a walk. The reason you do this is to avoid something called GDV (Gastric Dilatation-Volvulus).

GDV is often known as dog bloat, or a twisted stomach. It is caused by a number of things including large meals, stress, anxiety, excitement and vigorous exercise. It tends to be more common in larger dogs such as German Shepherds but it is worth bearing in mind for Poodles because some will eat their food extremely fast. This can impact the potential for GDV. If they are very fast easters you can reduce the amount they get fed in one sitting, and compensate by more frequent feeding.

GDV usually occurs within the first two hours of eating, and so the general rule has been to wait 30 minutes after feeding before taking them for a walk and to wait 30 minutes after a walk before feeding them (a gap between exercise and food of 30 minutes).

Some vets will recommend waiting for at least two hours after eating before you exercise them and to wait 30 minutes after exercise before feeding.

SLEEP

As mentioned earlier, puppies sleep a lot. When he is young and up to 3 months old, he can sleep 18 hours a day, sometimes up to 20!

He can fall asleep suddenly, and it can even appear as if he has fallen asleep mid-step. He will fall asleep with a chew in his mouth or just sit down in the middle of the floor and collapse. When he does, just pick him up and put him in his crate or basket (with the door open).

He should easily sleep for 7 hours at night, and some puppies can sleep for 7 hours without requiring a bathroom break.

Puppies need their sleep, so make sure you let him get it. This will be harder than you think in the first few weeks. There will be many visitors and lots of people who will want to pick him up and cuddle him. This is okay but don't forget his sleep time. He needs it.

Build this into your schedule so that it might look like this:

7:15 am - wake up and go outside for potty
7:30 am - breakfast
8:00 am - playtime
8:15 am - outside for toilet
8:20 am - sleep (with toy in the cage/depart for work?)
10:15 am - outside for toilet
10:30 - food
10:35 - outside for toilet
11:00 - playtime
11:15 - outside for toilet
11:20 am - sleep with Kong or Toy in the cage

1:15pm - wake up/ outside for toilet
1:20pm - food
1:25 - outside for toilet
2:00 - playtime
2:15 pm - outside for toilet
2:20 - sleep (cage with toy)

And so on. You will find a schedule that works for you as you discover when your puppy likes to go potty during the day. It might be after food or after playtime. But always take him out as soon as he awakens.

The timings will change as he gets a bit older and sleeps less.

Note that the schedule separates playtime from toilet time. I have mentioned this earlier in the book. You are aiming to distinguish between potty time and playtime.

You should aim to separate the activity in each outside visit when you are potty training him. You could, for example, wait until he potties before any play can start. After he potties and gets his praise and reward you can calmly wait for a minute and then signal the start of playtime. Try and mix playtime inside and out over the first few weeks so that he gets the hang of an outside visit being for potty time.

BEDTIME

You will find that your puppy will start to go to bed by himself as he gets used to your schedule, and he will soon fit in with your own bedtime.

In the early days, if he does wake up during the night, don't make a fuss and do not be tempted to play with him. He will be more than happy to play, but he needs to learn that this is not the right time. And don't turn on all the lights or it will seem like daytime to him. Take him outside to let him toilet and then return him to his bed.

Dogs should always have access to water but during his potty training at night time you may decide to remove his water bowl. Do this no more than 2 hours before he goes to bed, and make sure that he has had a recent drink first, he needs his water. This will help keep his bladder less active during the night.

MARKING

Male Poodles of all types can have a tendency to "mark" indoors. Marking is not the same as urinating in the home. It is normally territorial or a show of dominance. Fully-house trained dogs can mark - it is not a lack of potty training.

Your dog will leave small amounts of urine either in random places or in the same spot. Often the edges of couches or the legs of furniture. In my experience it can smell stronger than 'normal' urine.

Be vigilant and, if you see him marking, distract him and take him outside and reward him if he then toilets.

Marking in the home can often be a sign of stress and anxiety and can also be a hormonal response, not uncommon in intact males. The two most common reason are to show ownership or a sign of anxiety.

If your dog is not spayed or neutered (female dogs can mark too although it is less common), then neutering will reduce marking behaviour in 50-60% of cases.

Block access to the place where your dog is drawn to mark and if he has marked, the you need to clean it properly. Even if you think it is clean, your dog will be able to pick up the scent and keep re-marking in the same spot.

Check to see if there are other dogs in the area and close to the house. Sometimes you dog will be marking to put a 'stamp' on his territory.

Finally, stop and consider if he might be more anxious. Has anything changed? Is there new furniture in the house, is getting enough exercise, are there new people or animals around? Any of these things can cause him to mark and be cause him to be anxious.

CRATE TRAINING

Many people worry that using a crate might be cruel. If used properly, a crate is a place where your puppy will feel safe and happy - it will be his den. The main objective of your crate training is to teach him that the crate is his 'safe place' and that it belongs to him. Never use his crate as a 'sin bin'.

Using a crate will also bring with it a range of other benefits that will mean your life with your puppy can be as full and as engaging as possible - and it will allow him to be included in almost all of your activities, including vacations or holidays. Crate training is also often one of the best ways to help speed up house training.

The reason using the crate works for house training is that dogs don't like to mess where they sleep, and where they relax. Your puppy will not mess here, especially if you have crate trained him to view his crate as his safe place. What's more, if he is sleeping in his crate, he will do his very best to hold on until he can leave it.

This puts you in more control, because you will know where

your puppy is, and what he might want to do when you open the door, or when he leaves his crate, especially if he has been sleeping.

Remember, you will always take him outside to toilet as soon as he wakes up and it is a good idea to do this every time he leaves the crate if he has been in there for 20-30 minutes or more, even if he has not been sleeping.

Crate training has lots of other benefits. Your dog will be able to travel with you more easily and safely. You can visit friends and family more easily because you can use the crate as his portable bed. It also means that you can go out knowing that you won't return to chewed furniture or a general mess (the chewing usually only occurs with puppies), and your dog can use the crate as his bed during the day and during the night.

In summary, the crate gives your dog and puppy somewhere safe to rest and to sleep. It helps him feel comfortable when you leave the house; he can feel safe in a new house or room that you are visiting, and it means that he can enjoy more of your life outside of the home if you need to travel.

It will also help his settle with a dog sitter or if he needs to go and stay away from home when you go on vacation.

INTRODUCING YOUR PUPPY TO THE CRATE

After picking your crate, and before he arrives home, add a blanket or something soft for your puppy to lie on. Ideally add an item that has a familiar scent for his.

If you are using a second-hand crate, make sure you wash it thoroughly to remove any scent from the previous dog who may have been using it.

If you are using a wire crate, have something like a sheet or a blanket that you can place on top of it as well as around the sides. Don't cover up all four sides, and make sure the front of the crate (where the door is) is left uncovered. This can help to make it feel more like a den, especially at night.

Initially, you can place the crate in a room that is used by the rest of the household. This will help him get used to the crate without being separated from you and the rest of the family, and it will mean he doesn't feel alone and scared. A puppy will not be used to being alone, and it will make his anxious, especially when he first arrives home. Having company around him will be important.

If you want to, you can put the crate into the room that you want him to use and then follow the steps below. Once you pick your room make sure that you also spend lots of time with him there.

When your puppy comes home, place his toys, and, if you have not already done so, add the scented item from his previous home, into the crate.

The first stage is to place some food around the crate. If he doesn't start moving towards the crate, or being curious about it all by hisself, then entice his by calling his to the crate in a happy tone of voice, and by throwing tasty treats around and near the crate. Keep trying until he starts to come over to the crate and begins to feel comfortable around it.

The second stage is to slowly start moving the treats to the door, and then inside the crate. Give his lots of praise at all stages. Only start moving the treats inside the crate once he has started getting used to the outside of the crate. As he starts to enter the crate, don't close the door.

Keep playing the game and move the treats deeper into the crate. Just let his enter and leave and explore if he wants to. You want to get his used to entering and leaving by hisself.

It can take anything from 10 minutes to a few days, depending on his experience, to get him to go into his crate by himself. Keep the training sessions to between three and five minutes.

If, for any reason, your puppy is not responding to food or treats, then entice his with his favorite toy.

The third stage is to increase the length of time he spends in his crate. You can do this by feeding his in his crate, or you can put a Kong toy filled with treats into the cage, for his to play with.

If he is reluctant to go into the crate, put his food bowl beside the crate door, and then slowly move it into the crate until he eats at the back of the crate.

Once he is happy entering and leaving and lingering for a few minutes in his crate, try to close the door. You can do this when he is eating, but one of the most effective ways is to give him the Kong stuffed with something he loves.

Wait until he starts to become engrossed in getting his food out of the Kong, then slowly close the door. If you close the door and he gets anxious or scared, immediately open the door.

If he does nothing, then wait for a few minutes before opening the door again.

Keep increasing the length of time before you open the door. You are aiming to reach 10 minutes. If he shows any signs of distress, if he is panting, whining, cowering, or showing any signs of aggression, then you will know you have increased the time too quickly.

Once your puppy is happy to stay in the crate for up to 10 minutes after eating or playing, then you will know that he is now likely to understand that this crate is his safe space.

The last stage of his crate training can now begin, and this is when you move out of sight, while he is in his crate with the door closed.

This is the stage when his toys and his Kong (filled with food, peanut butter, or soft cheese) will really help.

Put his toys in his crate, and close the door once he has entered. Stay beside the crate for around five minutes before moving quietly from the room and out of sight.

Once you are out of sight, turn around and come back to the side of the crate and sit beside it for 5 minutes. Gradually start to stay out of sight longer. Do this throughout the day but at different times. You will need to repeat the process several times.

If you hear any barking or whining, do not come back mid bark or mid whine. Try and find a gap, and this is when you return. You are aiming to increase the time you are out of sight to around 30 minutes.

Once this has been achieved, you can start leaving the house altogether. But remember to provide toys for his to play with, so that he does not get bored. Before leaving, make sure he has had a small meal and has been exercised, and remember to leave calmly without any fuss.

In terms of sleeping at night, you can put the crate in your bedroom at overnight in the early days. You only want to do this for a few days and not any longer.

When your puppy first arrives home, he will have been used to sleeping with his brothers and sisters, so letting him sleep in his crate in your room will help him settle in.

Once you put the crate into the room where he will normally spend the night, make sure to turn out the lights when you (and he) go to bed. You can leave a low-level one on if you like, but make sure it isn't bright.

This will also mean that if you need to take him out during the night, he will recognize that this is sleep time. And don't forget that if you need to take him out during the night, don't turn on all the lights.

Types of Crate

There are 3 main types of crate. A plastic crate (or box), a wire crate or cage, and one made of fabric. I use the fabric case as a travel carry case and use it as a den when we are staying away from home overnight.

I use both a cage (in the house) and a fabric crate for travel, but I know many people who use a plastic crate. The choice is up to you.

What size of crate?

Unlike the crate's material, the size of the crate that you choose is important.

If the crate is too small, it will make your dog uncomfortable, and if it is too big, it can make your dog insecure. You need to know the height, width, and length of the crate.

The crate size will depend on both the weight and height of your puppy when he is fully grown.

The table below gives a general size and weight guide.

Finally, to save you from buying different crates as your puppy grows, you can section off a part of the crate with a separator to make it smaller when he is smaller.

RECOMMENDED CRATE SIZES:

Small Dog Breeds 24" Dog Crate (Toy)
Weight 11-25 lbs and 3"-17" in height.

Medium Dog Breeds 30" Dog Crate (Miniature)
Weight 26-40 lbs and 18"-19" in height.

Intermediate Dog Breeds 36″ Dog Crate (Miniature or Standard)

Weight 41-70 lbs and 20"-22" in height.

Large Dog Breeds 42″ Dog Crate (Standard)

Weight 71-90 lbs and 23" - 26" in height.

FOOD AND FEEDING

As we have discussed earlier, you need to get your puppy into a regular schedule. The quicker you can do this and get his used to this schedule, the easier everything becomes. Creating a schedule really can make a big difference.

Feeding them to the same schedule also means that they will want to relieve themselves in reaction to that schedule. This, in itself, will make it easier for you to house-train.

WHAT TO FEED THEM

Dogs are built to be meat-eaters, but they are descended from omnivores, so they can survive adequately without meat (if the protein balance is right).

The protein in meat is not the same as the protein found in plant-based foods, and this is one of the reasons to be careful of the food you give your puppy and your dog.

This doesn't mean that dogs can't live on a plant-based diet; it just means it will need to be supplemented with the essential proteins that he will require as well as Vitamin D.

Balancing nutrition is the most important aspect of your dogs' food. For example, we need our carbs for energy, but dogs don't need many carbs.

Dogs, and especially puppies, need fats and fatty acids. Most of these are contained in animal fats, but some seed and plant oils can provide a concentrated source of energy. You are looking for an Omega-3 family of essential fatty acids.

When looking for dog food, look at the type of calories rather than the overall total. For example, you don't want too much carbohydrate.

Today's average dog food can contain anywhere between 30% and 70% carbohydrates, but in the wild, dogs will intake only about 15%.

An adult dog's diet can contain up to 50% carbohydrate (by weight), up to 4.5% fibre, and a minimum of around 5.5% should come from fats, and 10% from protein.

You can read more about nutrition at nap.edu, and this is listed in the resources at the end of this book.

In general, though, if you want to check out how much meat is in your dog food, look at the ingredients list. The further down the meat appears, the lower the meat content.

The most common ingredients today are whole grain, fat, soya, and corn. So if you see chicken by-products, this doesn't mean it is chicken meat. It most likely isn't.

The top ingredients to look for (and look for a range of these in the same food) include deboned chicken or turkey, Atlantic mackerel and herring, chicken and turkey liver, chicken and turkey heart, and other items such as egg and other types of fish. All high in protein.

There has also been some debate about dry food versus wet food. The main difference being that wet food contains more water (around 75%) whereas dry food can contain only about 10% water.

Dry food tends to be more calorie-dense, and wet food has less grain and fewer carbs. Grain isn't necessarily a bad thing, it just depends on quantity.

Dry food lasts for longer and tend to be more cost-effective than wet food.

There are lots of choices on the market, and you will want to research this for yourself.

It's important to vary their food and its texture from time-to-time to give them a little change. Like many smaller dogs, Poodles can be fussy eaters so varying their diet (and sometimes portion size) can keep them engaged and interested in their food. You may also discover something that they love and decide to stick with it.

Some owners also like to feed their dog a raw diet known as RAW or a BARF diet (Bones and Raw Food). There are quite a few sites online that can explain how to do this and what this diet includes. A key to this diet is balance and The Natural Dog site (A Guide to Raw Diet and Health The Natural Way) is a good place to start if this is something that you are interested in finding more about.

HOW MUCH TO FEED

Puppies can require up to double the energy intake of adult dogs. This is based on the weight of your puppy - it doesn't mean they eat twice as much as an adult dog, just that per pound of weight they do.

Depending on your type of Poodle, they will reach their adult weight anywhere between 5 and 14 months old. You can check the table in Chapter 2 for the expected size and weight.

Although Poodles can be fussy eaters they also love to eat - probably as a result of their constant energy. It can mean that it is best to control their feeding and not leave food in their bowl for them to nibble on between meals.

The frequency really does depend on how old they are. A puppy's tummy is small and it grows over time. This means that you need to feed smaller amounts more regularly, the younger they are.

Puppies aged 8-16 weeks need to be fed 4 meals a day, perhaps every 3 hours. Pups ages 3 to 6 months should be fed 3 times a day (every 4 hours) and then after that twice a day, in the morning and early evening.

Your aim is to spread their nutrition throughout the day, so space out the times to equal intervals across the day. Once you are taking your puppy out for walks, which will mean more exercise, remember not to feed your puppy just before or after exercise.

The amount that you feed your puppy will depend on their weight and age. The dog food you choose will also have a variety of different protein levels.

When you decide on your dog food, the packaging will tell you how much to feed your puppy (depending on their weight). If you are in any doubt, ask your veterinarian.

DANGEROUS FOODS FOR YOUR DOG

Alcohol - under no circumstances give your dog alcohol. Alcohol contains ethyl alcohol (ethanol) which is a seriously toxic chemical that affects the central nervous, motor response and respiratory system. In the worst-case scenario, alcohol can cause death. Contact your vet right away and do not induce vomiting.

Chocolate and **cocoa** contain the chemical theo-bromide which effects the heart, lungs, kidney and central nervous system. Because the toxicity is based on the purity of the chocolate, dark chocolate, including cooking chocolate, is the worst. A medium size dog can be affected by just 6 small squares of cooking chocolate, but it would take nearly ¾ lb. of milk chocolate to have the same affect. If your puppy or dog has eaten dark chocolate contact your vet immediately. You will be asked the weight of your dog so its useful to always check his weight regularly. Symptoms include seizures, vomiting, diarrhoea, excitement, tremors, abnormal heart rate/rhythm, staggering, and even coma.

Caffeine —don't give your puppy anything with caffeine. Things that can include caffeine are obviously coffee, but chocolate can also contain caffeine. Caffeine has a similar effect as chocolate.

Coconut (including coconut oil) - might cause stomach upsets, but coconut water should not be given to your dog.

Onion, chives, and **garlic** can irritate the bowel and are toxic to dogs. The thiosulphate these contain can cause Heinz body anaemia, which causes destruction of red blood cells leading to eventual kidney damage. Dogs don't have the liver enzyme necessary to digest them. The amount required will depend on body weight. It is toxic in raw, cooked or dried form.

Nuts and Cherry, peach, apricot and plum stones naturally contain cyanide. Cyanide poisoning has classic symptoms of vomiting, skin irritation, laboured breathing, apnoea tachycardia, cardiac arrhythmias, and eventually coma. Urgent vet treatment is required. In addition the leaves, fruit, seeds and bark of avocados contain Persin, which will cause vomiting and diarrhoea. (Pecans, Almonds, Walnuts, Macadamia) - these have the potential to not only cause vomiting but possible pancreatitis.

Raisins and grapes - avoid giving your dog raisins or grapes. The effect the toxins have is still not definitive, but it can cause Kidney failure. This also includes other dried variants like sultanas and currants and any foods containing grape, such as grape juice, raisin cereal, raisin bread, granola, trail mix, and raisin cookies or bars. Early signs are vomiting, diarrhoea, and lethargy. One of the most common causes is from your dog eating wild bird food. Ground feeders should be enclosed which only allow birds to enter.

Raw Potato and unripe tomato's are poisonous to dogs. The tomato plant contains atropine and the potato contains solanine (which has an atropine-effect). This causes gastrointestinal problems. Symptoms to look for are blurred vision, vomiting, diarrhoea, low temperature, and slow heart rate. More serious symptoms are tremors, seizures, and a decreased heart rate. In both instances the dog will require vet treatment.

Bones - Generally speaking, be careful of any bones that you give your dog to chew. Avoid cooked bones because they tend to splinter and they can puncture their digestive tract if they swallow these splinters. If they can easily break a bone apart (raw or cooked), they can lodge in their throats or their intestines. They love bones so just pick your bone carefully.

Shellfish - some dogs are okay with shellfish, but one of my dogs will vomit immediately, and this will happen with even small traces of shellfish such as prawns or langoustine. This doesn't mean dogs can't eat fish. They can eat fish, and fish is good for them in many cases. Always ensure it is cooked and sufficiently cooled.

Xylitol (sweetener) and all foods containing Xylitol is toxic to dogs. It can cause your dog's blood sugar to drop and cause acute liver failure and even death. Early symptoms include vomiting, lethargy, and coordination problems or seizures.

Xylitol is used as a sweetener in several products including candy, gum, baked goods, diet foods, and even some peanut butter and toothpaste.

What to do if your pet is poisoned

These are the instructions from the Pet Poison helpline:-

- Remove your pet from the area.

- Check to make sure your pet is safe: breathing and acting normally.
- Do NOT give any home antidotes.
- Do NOT induce vomiting without consulting a vet or Pet Poison helpline.
- Call Your Vet or, in the US, the Pet Poison helpline.
- If veterinary attention is necessary, contact your veterinarian or emergency veterinary clinic immediately.

Bear in mind that it is always better when a toxicity is reported immediately, so don't wait to see if your dog becomes symptomatic before calling for help. There is a narrow window of time when your puppy can be decontaminated (induced vomiting or pumping the stomach) in the case of a poisoning.

CHEWING AND MOUTHING

Puppies not only chew but there is a period when they will use their mouths - a lot! This is called mouthing, and their tiny teeth are remarkably sharp.

They will grab your trouser legs or put their mouth around your hands - and their sharp teeth will take your breath away.

Puppies need to learn about different textures - and human skin is just one of the textures they need to learn about. They also need to understand how hard they can close their jaws, and when enough is enough. They can only learn this by doing it. If you have children then you need to be very aware of this.

MOUTHING

All puppies will go through this phase, and you will want to teach them about 'bite inhibition'.

This is something that puppies, who have come from a larger litter, will have learned a bit about, because they usually learn this through play with their litter mates (and socialization classes can help too).

There were many times when we had a litter and heard squeals of outrage or pain, as they pushed each other over and mouthed at ears, paws, and anything they could get their tiny mouths around.

When one of the pups squealed, they would stop playing, but so did the protagonist. That pup nipping tended to look as surprised as the pup that got a sharp tooth implanted into it. Yet, just a few moments later, they were back playing.

It was notable that the pup that got the painful nip was pretty eager to try this out on one of the other unsuspecting puppies.

This is just part-and-parcel of a puppy growing up and learning boundaries. But it doesn't make it easier or any less painful. However, over time, puppies learn to understand each other and know how hard a bite they can get away with. The screams of surprise between them always becomes less frequent.

Puppies are most likely to try and mouth you when you are playing with them, tickling their tummy, or petting them.

Nor surprisingly, the best way to deal with mouthing is to behave like a puppy.

First of all - it's important to let your puppy mouth you.

Let him have your hand. When he closes his mouth too hard, and his sharp teeth become painful, squeal like a puppy or use the word "stop" and then stop playing with him. Just let your hand go limp so that it is no fun to play with.

This should stop your puppy for a moment or two. He will be just as surprised as you. When he relaxes his mouth and stops, then praise him. Then let him have your hand again.

He will definitely go too far quite a few times, so just keep repeating over a 15- or 20-minute time intervals until he learns how hard he can close his mouth without hurting you.

If your squealing and "stop' doesn't work, then put him on the "naughty step' so to speak. Stop playing with him for 30 seconds or so. After this, start playing with him again.

If he does it again, then repeat, and if this still doesn't work, then move away from him as soon as he mouths you and you feel that nip.

As the hard biting stops, you will want to continue teaching him as he moves his mouthing levels down from sore to moderate. Slowly teaching him not to mouth at all.

Eventually, he will know exactly the level of pressure that he can safely apply when he is playing.

Whatever you do, don't hit your puppy for mouthing. This will only make him play harder, but it may also cause him to fear you.

Remember not to jerk your hands away from your puppy when he starts mouthing you. He still thinks this is a game and is more likely to lunge forward. Likewise, don't wave your hands in front of his face for the same reason - he will think that this is a game too.

Once you have done this, you want him to learn not to mouth at all on human skin, and to let you pet him without being mouthed.

When your puppy tries to mouth you when you are petting them, distract him by giving him a treat or a chew toy. I ended up using a tug toy. Wave it in front of him and just said, "Play Tug."

This worked really well because he used to follow me around and grab my ankles to get me to play with him. To stop his doing this I would stand still and say, "play tug." It's classic distraction training!

When he stopped trying to grab my ankles, I would praise him. Eventually, I could walk around without being tailed by a puppy with sharp teeth.

One last thing to bear in mind. Like all toddlers, puppies can have tantrums. I know a Poodle who really likes her tantrums! Her body will be stiffer, and her mouth might be tighter around the lips.

If you notice this while you are playing with your puppy, just stop the play.

Don't squeal if he bites you (it will be harder than normal). If you are holding him, stop playing but continue to hold him for a few seconds, then let him go.

Don't make him afraid of you, you just want him to know that he has gone too far. If you notice that your puppy continues to have tantrums, you will need to get more help from a professional.

CHEWING

Most dogs like to chew, and some breeds are more likely to chew than others. For example, Labradors and Staffordshire Bull Terriers tend to have a stronger desire to chew. Because Poodles are intelligent with moderate-to-high energy, they need a lot of mental stimulation and if they are bored, they will be inclined to chew.

All puppies enjoy and need to chew. They do this to explore their environment and understand the texture of things; they don't have hands, and they like to pick things up. So the only way that he can explore is to use his mouth.

All puppies go through the teething phase which also causes chewing. Depending on your Poodle, he will start to experience discomfort in his mouth as his teething process gets underway anywhere between four and eight months. He will chew to help remove his baby teeth, and he will chew to help with the pain of his adult teeth erupting in his gums.

• 4 Months old - the incisors begin to grow in
• 5 months old - the canine teeth begin to grow in
• 6 months old - the molars begin to grow in
• By 8 months old, a puppy should have all teeth ascended and stop teething. Some Poodles will be later than this and teething may last a bit longer.

As your puppy starts to reach adolescence, his chewing is going to get worse. Thise are two possible reasons for this.

It is around now that he will tend to get easily bored so try to find new games (especially mental exercise games) and games to keep him occupied.

It is also around this time that his adult teeth are settling into the jaw, which can be uncomfortable for some dogs.

Whatever the reason, and it might be both of the above reasons, your puppy is going to chew at things.

In my case, it was furniture. This included the legs of tables, the sides of the sofa, shoes, wallets, and spectacles.

You will need to teach everyone in your household to put their shoes out of reach, and preferably out of sight, along with any toys that have different textures.

There will be the favored chew items. Puppies love shoes - they are just about the right consistency of hard and soft making them perfect for exploring different textures. Much the same as furniture too.

Don't forget that your puppy might chew all of his life (mine stick to tennis balls now), but it will never be as bad as that first year. Dogs chew when they get older because it relaxes them and it's a calming activity (and they enjoy it).

Here are some chew toys and tips that might help.

• Try and change your dog's chew toys regularly by rotating them every few days. This will prevent him from getting bored and prevent him from looking for something else to chew that might look more interesting.

• Remove anything that you don't want him to chew and keep everything well out of reach. I lost a TV remote control and a pair of glasses by forgetting to move them to higher ground.

• If you find your puppy chewing on something that is not allowed, don't punish him or shout at him. This will only make him anxious. Instead, simply distract his attention and then direct him to a chew toy that you want him to play with. When he starts to play with it, make a fuss of him.

• Don't forget to remove anything dangerous to your puppy when he cannot be supervised. This includes some types of household plants (see below for some examples) that are poisonous to dogs. And watch out for wires that run along the floor.

• Many hard plastic toys are not made for chewing by a dog. The best chew toys are made of the type of hard rubber that you get with your Kong. You can also consider activity balls (like Kong's, you can place kibble, cheese spread, peanut butter, or other treats or food inside). Ropes are also good but avoid nylon or anything that he can pull apart into a string.

• Chews such as dental chews or edible chews can distract your puppy - but they can be eaten quite quickly. Test which chews your puppy likes the most and which ones last the longest.

• Keep all house plants well out of reach, especially the ones that are poisonous to dogs. For example Cyclamen, Poinsettia, some Lilly's, Oleander, Brunfelsia, Aloe, Amaryllis (bulbs), Azalea, Cyclamen, Water Hemlock. You can find a list on the DogsTrust website.

TRAINING AT HOME

You will need a few tools and some equipment to progress with training and these are outlined below. You will also start by training some basic cues in the house and in the garden before you start taking your puppy outside for walks. It is always a good idea to cover the basics at home. First of all you need to have a few items and systems in place.

Treats

Treats are the mainstay of dog training at the puppy stage, but you should also introduce other rewards such as toys and praise. In a few cases dogs can prefer toys to treats.

Some people cut up hot dogs, I made something called liver cake, and one of the simplest things to do is to grab a handful of his kibble and use this as a dog training treat. You will need a selection of 3 or 4 different treats because you will want to adopt a value-reward system.

Value-Reward System

A value-reward approach means that you will reward a type of treat based on how difficult the task is that you are asking your puppy to do. Kibble, for example, is often not as highly valued as cheese or a piece of hot dog or a carrot. This means that your puppy will like kibble, but he will like a hot dog more and he will love a small bit of cheese, and he will adore a little bit of liver cake.

In this example, he would get what he loves most when he accomplishes something difficult or that he has never done before. You will then use this knowledge to reward based on difficulty, the more difficult the higher the reward value.

This allows you to reward on value and depending on what you want him to do. You will use this for recall training too - the faster he returns the higher the value of reward. It means that you can use the treat (and later, the reward) that matches his effort.

For example, if he absolutely loves cheese then save this as a special treat when he does something for the first few times. If he has already learned to sit, then offer him kibble when he sits. Try not to move from high value to low value as soon as he learns to sit, gradually move down the value chain to kibble. This process can also increase the connection between you and your puppy. Don't forget that you will be praising him all the time.

There are a few reasons that treats might not work. They might not be tasty enough, he might be too stressed or he might get his treats all the time so he doesn't realize what the reward means - this is known as over-reinforcement. It's also possible that your puppy might not be hungry. Try and train him on an empty stomach but not right before he is due to be fed - if a puppy is too hungry then all that his mind will be concentrating on is food and he won't be able to concentrate on his training.

Over reinforcement, which simply means using treats too often, is common. This can be hard to get right but using the value reward system can help. Over-time, rather than getting kibble for example he will get lots of praise and no treat, or his treat might be to do something he loves (play or get the ball) as well as lots of praise.

You are eventually aiming to have the desired behavior with no treats at all and this also helps because you won't always be able to have a treat in your hand.

Harness

Collars and choke collars are no longer thought to be good for dogs. They can be worn in the house but a harness should be used for training - especially leash and recall. Training is all about trust, and restrictive items just won't build the trust you are looking for.

Leash

Avoid using a flexible leash. They won't give you the control that you need and they get tangled up in legs including yours or someone else's in the park and on the street. You will ideally use a long-leash (around 25ft-30ft in length). This is known as a long-line. You will also want a shorter training leash of around 4ft and you can use this as his day-leash or 'normal' leash.

Whistles and Clickers

Almost all leash training will involve using a clicker - I train with and without a clicker. Whistles are great for recall especially for dog breeds that like to explore and good for your Standard Poodle.

With clicker training, this must always be followed with a reward, for example, click-treat. This is known as the primary and secondary enforcer.

Toys

You are going to use your puppy's toys during recall training. You are aiming to get him to leave a toy and come to you when he is called. You will have a treat so that he sees the value of leaving his toy and coming to you instead.

BASIC TRAINING

You can begin basic training over the first few weeks that your puppy is home by teaching him the basic commands that you will use throughout his life.

Always keep the training sessions to between 5 and 10 minutes. If he comes up against something he can't do, then return to something that he can do.

You always want him to enjoy the training session so if he gets stuck, take him back a step so that, at the end of the session as well as during it, he is happy and receives his praise and reward - it is important to end the session on a positive note.

I will mention using hand signals during some of the training in the following pages, and you should try to use this type of training as much as you can, rather than only verbal cues. Use both if you don't feel comfortable with only hand signals.

Reinforcement (a part of operant conditioning) and using body language rather than verbal cues is now considered as the foundation for good dog training. Reinforcement is rewarding without a treat i.e. by using praise and offering your puppy something else he loves (a toy or to go and play).

Getting to know his name

Always reward your puppy when he responds to his name. It doesn't matter how or why he responds to his name, it only matters that he does, and you need to reward his for doing so. You will start to do this as soon as he arrives home.

Whenever you say his name and he looks at you, even if it was an accidental look, reward him.

Don't ever be tempted to use his name as punishment because he won't understand and he will be confused by your use of his name and by your annoyance.

Paying Attention

The next stage is to teach him to look at you and you will do this before you start taking your puppy outdoors for walks. I know dogs that, to this day, don't make eye contact with their owner. It is an often overlooked training activity and yet it is a hidden gem in terms of getting your puppy, and later your grown-up dog's, attention and it will make his training much easier.

It will mean that, even if your puppy starts to get engrossed or fixated on something, you can get his attention back to you, and you can change his focus to you, to stop him doing whatever it was that he was doing. I find this particularly useful for leash training.

To do this he needs to want to pay attention to you.

You will already have started training him to look at you during the period you were teaching him his name, but now you want to actively encourage it and to repeat the process in many different locations and environments. You will say his name, he needs to look at you and as soon as he makes eye contact, then you can reward him with click-treat, or with praise and reward, and the reward could be a treat or to play with a toy.

A game is the best way to train your Poodle puppy to look at you.

To play the game, sit down with your puppy with a handful of treats in your pocket. Make sure that you are sitting so that you are close to him, but so that he needs to look up to see your eyes.

Take out a treat and get his attention. Place the treat between your eyes. Your puppy will follow the treat all the way to your head and eyes. As soon as there is eye-contact, even briefly, give him the treat.

In the beginning, the eye contact might be an accident on his part but that's okay. If he gets rewarded for it, he will soon learn. Keep repeating until he always has eye contact with you. If he doesn't look at you at first, then help his find your eyes so that he knows what he is supposed to do.

Once he knows what the game is and is responding in the way that you want, start putting the treat behind your head or neck and so that he can't see the treat. Again, as soon as there is eye contact - but not before - give him the treat.

The next part of this game is to start using his name. Do exactly the same process but as you place the treat between your eyes, say his name. You will need to do all this quite quickly to link the eye contact with the name call and his reward but he will get there.

He now knows that when you say his name you want him to look at you, and he will want to pay attention to you because there will be a reward coming!

THE FUNDAMENTAL CUES

You will begin teaching your puppy what you mean by the recall cue. I will use the example of 'come'. The important part is to always use the same word and use it only when you want him to come to you.

Don't mix it into other cues. This one word means one thing, and one thing only - to come to you.

You will adopt this rule for all his cues. Make sure each one is unique to the action expected and can't be confused with other cues. For example, don't use 'come here' if 'here' is used as another cue that needs a different action.

Start your training in the house then move to enclosed areas with few distractions.

Sit

There are a few ways to teach your puppy to sit, but I have used this one to the best effect.

Sit down beside your puppy holding a treat, then put the treat in front of his nose, slowly lifting it above his head. As he tilts his head up to follow the treat, he is likely to sit as he tries to reach the treat.

You say the word 'sit' just before his bottom touches the ground. Then, as soon as his bottom touches the ground, reward him with the treat. Your puppy is learning the word sit but also starting to recognize your hand signal i.e. the movement of your arm.

Keep doing this, eventually removing the treat from your hand but using your hand as a signal or cue to get him to sit, and saying the word 'sit' as you raise your hand to the sitting position. Always reward him as soon as he sits down.

Don't try to push his bottom to the ground to get him to sit - it rarely works.

Lie Down

For some reason, this is the fastest command to teach when you do it like this, and your puppy will be lying down within one training session.

Simply take out his treat and hold it to his nose, then move it down slowly to the floor (I usually say 'Lie' at this point too rather than wait until later in training). Slide the treat on the floor away from him. He will start to move down.

As soon as he is almost down (he won't lie down right away, and his bottom is likely to remain in mid-air), gave him the treat.

Keep doing this and getting him to move further into the lie position (you can keep dragging the treat towards you on the floor as this can often help).

Reward and praise him each time. Eventually, you will only

give him the treat when he is fully down. By now, he will be used to your hand moving down and hearing the phrase 'Lie'.

Training sit-stay

To teach your dog to stay, first of all, ask him to sit. Then hold up your hand so that your palm is straight in front of him and directed towards his face (but not in any kind of threatening way).

Take a step backward so that you are facing him and with your palm facing him and say 'stay'. If he stays for even a few seconds, come back to him and reward him.

Do this a few times and then take a few more steps backward increasing the distance, then walk back to his and reward him. Keep repeating moving further away.

Your puppy is learning that not only is he getting rewarded but that you come back to him. Start to move to different positions so that you are to each side and eventually behind him. If he gets up, just move back to him and give him praise then try again.

You will need to repeat this in several different locations aeon the house and in the garden. As he starts to get better at this, begin to introduce him to areas with more distractions, or create distractions like more people of other dogs he knows, and start moving behind objects so that he can't see you. Try and do this everywhere you go.

Every time after that, when your puppy sits try and remember to praise/reward his as he will build this into a behavior default. One that he will enjoy, feels safe with, and knows will bring praise/reward.

The 'come' cue

I know of someone who began basic recall in their hallway, which was ideal for ensuring their puppy was set up for success during the early training because there were limited directional options, and little distraction. This is important. Remember that you want to ensure that your puppy always succeeds and this might mean you need to adapt things to make sure that he can succeed through each step of his training.

Once you have decided on your location, show your puppy his favorite treat or toy, and as he comes towards you to get his toy or treat (don't ask his to come to you, let him do it by himself), praise him and reward him as he reaches you. Do this a few times.

Once again, add some distraction. One fun way to do this is to have other family members or friends in a room with you. As you walk towards them and he starts to get interested in this curious and fun distraction, quickly run away and call him so that he chases you.

Encourage him to catch up and when he does, he will of course get his treat and probably a big cuddle as an extra reward.

Like many of the training games you can play with him, mix them up so that he doesn't always know what to expect. It will keep him even more interested in what you are about to get up to next. And don't forget to get other family members to lead the training too.

After a few times of playing this game, start to add in his cue so that he gets used to it. As he starts coming towards you to get his toy (and ideally looks at you), add in the cue you have chosen. In my example, 'Come'.

Combine sit, stay and come

Finally, combine the 'come' cue with the 'sit and stay' cue.

This was the main recall training I started with Millie indoors when she was around 12 weeks old and it was very effective.

Ask your puppy to sit, and then ask him to stay - I also held my hand up as a 'stay' visual cue..

Walk backwards a few steps while facing your puppy - I kept holding my hand up as I was walking away.

The difference now is that you want him to come to you following the sit-stay. If he stays for just a few seconds, ask him to come and give him a treat when he comes to you.

Keep repeating this and do it at the start of every training session. As he starts to get good at this, start to move further and further away and eventually try walking away with your back to his.

Like all of his training, build up the distance and the distractions to this game - but if you go too far and he starts to come towards you too soon, just go back a few steps to the point at which it was working and then keep trying to build the distance.

The next stage is to go outside but not for a 'proper' walk just yet. You can go for a walk on-leash but not off-leash.

Summary and the 10 steps for basic recall

1. Decide on your location (hallway, kitchen, etc) - and later, vary the location

2. Show your puppy his favorite toy or a treat but don't call him, let him come to you

3. When he gets to you give him the treat along with praise

4. Repeat

5. Start adding your recall cue ('come', visual cue or whistle) as he starts coming towards you

6. Reward him when he gets to you

7. Repeat steps 5 and 6

8. When he comes to you give him the treat then ask him to sit and give his another treat

9. Repeat this until he knows what to do

10. Ask him to sit and stay, walk away from him (initially

walking backwards so that you are facing him) and then use his cue to come to you

11. When he gets to you give him the treat along with praise

12. Repeat the recall and sit and stay in other locations and start to add in distractions

Leash training

You can start putting his lead on in the house so that he gets used to it. As soon as his leash is clipped on, give him a treat. Have another treat in your hand and use this to get him to walk beside you.

To do this, hold the treat just in front of his nose, loosely cupped in your hand, so that your palm is facing his nose with your arm hanging down beside you.

He will move towards your hand as you start taking a few steps forward which makes him move and walk along beside you. Build this up slowly and for no more than 5 minutes at a time at the start.

Eventually, walk a few paces, then turn in the opposite direction getting him to follow you.

Repeat this process of walking a few steps and turning.

RECALL TRAINING

In this chapter we will outline the main training you will start doing with your puppy as you prepare, and then, start taking his out for walks.

CUES

Dogs train better when they are making their own choices - especially Poodles. You want him to want to make the choice to come to you, when you ask him. This means that you must never be angry when he comes back to you, no matter how long it has taken.

You are aiming to have your dog return to you on cue no matter how many other exciting things are going on around him. This means that your puppy needs to want to return to you on cue, not only when there are no other dogs around, but also when there are dogs to play with.

You can only achieve this if you are more interesting than whatever else he is doing, and if he is listening and paying attention to you.

In summary, you want him to stop what he is doing; you want him to look at you, and you want him to come to you on cue.

INTRODUCING THE RECALL CUE

Most people use the word 'come' or 'here' as their vocal cue for their recall. Some might use a whistle. I mix a verbal and visual cue. Once you have decided on the word you want to use, then you must keep it. Consistency is vital for your dog to understand what you mean.

You will start using this early and you will have begun this training in the house. You will use this cue for many reason. When you want him to come for his dinner you will use it, and when you are going to give him a big cuddle or play with him, you will use it.

The outcome of his action when he hears the word and responds correctly means he feels great because he gets something he loves and he gets lots of praise from you. In dog training language, he is building a positive association with the word.

Try to build in hand signals too - I tend to open my arms as a visual cue to come.

Like most training sessions, keep the training to around 10 minutes and watch out for any signs that he is getting stressed (quick head movements, grabbing the treat/food, ears flat) and try not to get him over-excited.

If your puppy is a part of a household then get all members involved in the training too. Don't forget to ask him to do something you know he can do at the end of the training so that it ends in success. You want him to enjoy his training.

You will have already introduced him to training at home including the basic 'sit', 'stay, and 'come' cues. You will now begin leash and recall training in preparation for his daily walks and exercise in the park.

You won't let him off leash outside in an unenclosed area until you are happy that he will return to you.

To do this you need to introduce him to different locations and train him in these locations - different rooms in the house, different areas of the garden or different areas of an enclosed area. You will then introduce lots of distractions as the training develops - a toy, another person, another dog that you know (and that you know is vaccinated) etc and you will keep doing the training exercises with all these distractions present.

You are aiming to get him to always pay attention to you and to always return to you despite any exciting activity or scents that he might be interested in - and if he can get used to this in a safe garden then he will be familiar with what to do once he gets to the park.

When it comes to recall, you should wait until his recall is up to about 70%-80% before you start adding the distraction element of his recall training.

SIT STAY RELEASE

Sit Stay is one of the most important cues your dog will learn and the ones you will use most often.

You will want to use both verbal and visual cues. Your visual cue for 'stay' will be holding up your hand, but without raising your arm above your head - just hold it in front of you and direct your palm to your puppy's face. This is his visual cue for stay.

The verbal cue would be 'Stay'. Visual cues are also a good way of helping your dog focus on you.

Normally the first part is to ask your puppy to 'sit' then this is followed by 'stay' (or 'wait').

By this stage (by the time you are going for outside walks) you will have trained your puppy to 'sit' and will have practiced some 'stay' in the home or garden. We have covered this earlier.

You will now start to use the sit cue for a variety of reasons. In the car, when you go to the door, when you are at a crosswalk, and so on. This means you need to train him to sit but you also need to let him know when it's okay to move forward.

To do this, start by having him on his leash. Get him to sit (and reward) then decide on your cue for 'let's go' this can be 'let's go' or 'ok go' or whatever you choose. Say your cue and move a few steps and praise him, ask him to sit and reward.

Begin with short distances (a few steps) to get him used to the 'ok go' cue. Repeat the process of 'sit', reward 'ok go' reward, walk a few steps then repeat. This is known as the release cue.

This can mean that the release cue is seen as a reward too because when he comes back he then gets to go and have fun again. It also means that he will learn that coming back doesn't mean the end of the play.

Finally, some trainers consider recall to include holding your puppy's collar when he returns as full recall and they use it before the release cue. The puppy comes back, he sits and the collar is taken then the reward is given. This is followed by the release cue.

Some are happy with only the sit. This really is up to you but I prefer the collar hold as it gives you more control should you ever need it.

TRAINING OUTSIDE

Training for recall outside of the house is vital. It is here that he is going to find the most distractions. You must make sure that the area you choose is fully enclosed. Just like the early days of house training, you will start with very few distractions.

This is when you are going to work with the clicker and training leads and when you will start working out the value that he attaches to each of his different treats if you haven't already done so.

A great tip is to train your puppy before he has eaten - this means the treat you are offering will be of higher value to him and he will be more interested in them! And don't train him for too long. Pay attention if he looks like he is getting bored and stop the training and start again the next day.

To get started, put your puppy in his harness and on his training leash. Just like the early indoor training, you can start with rewarding an action with no other cues, to get him used to the long-line and outdoor training. He will know what to do quickly, because he has already been trained indoors.

The difference now is that you are going to place something he might want to eat or might want to get (a toy), a short distance away from him, and within the length of the leash, or just a bit further away. You are now introducing something he wants to get to but that is away from you.

As he goes towards the object or the treat (but not too tasty), tighten his leash and say his name then the cue e.g., Barney 'come'. As soon as he turns and comes (even if it's only a step or two) reward and praise him.

If you are using a clicker, you will click as soon as he turns. Aim to have an even tastier treat for him than the one he was going towards. You want to increase the value of the treats the more you want him to do something, so that he prefers to choose that tastier treat.

By having the leash on him, you can also gently encourage him to come towards you to get his reward if you need to. The leash helps you have a bit of control over this recall in the early stages as he continues to establish the cue 'come' outside of the house, and where he will want to explore more.

You will also play on the training leash and long line. Give him a few treats then run forward or backward a few steps and say 'Barney, Come!' in a playful voice while holding a treat out at the height of his nose (so that all of his feet are on the ground) and as he reaches you give him the treat.

You can extend this game to add the sit. As he reaches you to get his treat, move the treat up in front of his nose, so that he is forced back into the sit position to get his treat. In this way the come and sit are the same cue which means when you ask him to come, he will come to you and sit without being asked to sit.

You can, and should start practicing this as soon as you can. Puppies learn most up to the age of 18 weeks.

The next step for recall training is to have his move further away from you, and for him to return when he hears his cue. Good recall means he does this all the time. If he is not, then he is not ready, and you won't want to risk letting him off-leash. You will have already trained him to come and you are now continuing to establish this outside of the home.

To understand what you are asking your puppy to do, think about it like this. He is exploring and having fun, he is finding interesting and exciting things to sniff and play with. When you call him, you want him to prefer to come to you rather than keep doing whatever he is enjoying. If you can achieve this, then there is no reason for him not to return to you when called.

To do this you will want to start including training games. You will have worked out what his favorite treats are, and which ones top the list. Cheese, hotdog, carrot, kibble - my dogs love cheese and I used to make liver cake which they absolutely loved. It was probably the single reason Millie's recall and leash training went so well.

USING THE LONG-LINE

You don't need to use the long-line but it can be really helpful and, if you can, I would recommend it. To describe how this is done I picked a hand but you will end up doing something that works for you.

Practice this in a garden if you can, and, in the beginning, have no other distractions. You want to get used to working with the long line and you also want to test that your training is working.

Hold the end of the line in your right hand so that you have it tightly held. Wrap the length of the line into loops so that you can slowly release the line over the front of your body, feeding it through your left hand, making sure it can be easily released.

In your left hand, you are holding the part of the line that is acting as your dog leash, and it is attached to his harness, and your hand is operating as a feeder, controlling the delivery of the line.

This means you can slowly release the line through your left hand, to allow your puppy to move away from you, or clamp it closed (gently) to slow or stop the release of the line.

You will have your right hand holding the end of the long line as well as the loops of the spare line. Once you are comfortable you can start the training.

Slowly move in a circle on the same spot so that he is running around you, loosening the line so that he can move away from you, and then call him back to you. Just get him used to the leash and watching you, and knowing that he gets a reward when he comes back.

You can then add a game (and later you can play this off-leash too), by throwing a treat away from you, and letting your puppy go towards the treat.

Once he has eaten his treat, call his name to get his attention, wait until he looks at you (click), 'come' (cue), and when he comes to you (praise/reward). Then throw another treat in a different direction so that he is constantly running away and towards you in a fun game.

When you need to tighten or 'pull' the line to encourage him to come back on his cue, move or lean forward rather than move against him, and gently make the line shorter. This allows you to be in control of your puppy whilst letting him return without feeling 'pulled'.

The final part is to wait until he is preoccupied with something and is not looking at you. Get his attention and ask him to come. If he comes then praise and reward. If he doesn't come, just walk to him and show him all the treats you have, and then walk away from him.

He is likely to follow you to try and get a treat. Just ignore him. As soon as he isn't right beside you, ask him to come to you. When he does, give his lots of praise and a favorite treat. It won't take long for him to realise that coming is much better than not coming.

The next step is to repeat the indoor sit stay come training in the outdoor environment. Just as you did indoors get your puppy to sit-stay and then move away from him while still facing him and then ask him to 'come'. e.g., 'Barney, come'. Slowly build the distance all the while using the long line.

The next two steps are new, and before you can try off-leash outdoor you want to introduce the 'let's go' or 'let's play' cue which combines the sit-stay.

Ask him to sit-stay beside you, then use your release cue, 'let's go', and start walking. As he moves away and then moves ahead of you, call him back to you (click on a turn of the head towards you), as he starts coming towards you, you might want to encourage him (I held my arms open), reward him when he gets to you, then ask him to sit (reward).

The last step is to practice off-leash - again, you will do this in a space that is enclosed and where he will be safe. Simply let him wander away from you and then call his to you using your cue. Be exciting and have a treat ready for him. Try and keep his attention on you as he comes to you - make a noise or hold your arms open - you want him to be focused on you.

Don't keep repeating the cue or start raising your voice if he doesn't come. This will confuse him, and he won't be able to understand what his cue word is, eventually tuning it out which means he just won't hear it.

If you raise your voice, he won't think that coming to you is going to be lots of fun. Eventually, it could have the opposite effect, and he won't want to come at all.

RANDOM AND VARIABLE REINFORCEMENT

The best way to train your puppy is using random and variable reinforcement. All this means is that over time change how often he gets a treat for the same behavior, so that he is hoping for it each time (don't wait too long to reward as you start to reduce the level of treats) and change the value of the treat (for a really good response).

If you want to, you can measure the average response time for recall (either daily or per 12 returns, etc.) so that when he comes back faster, he gets a super tasty treat. This is the most effective way to train your puppy to become addicted to coming back to you.

One last trick - if your puppy has taken a while to return on cue then, when he arrives, show him the treat and put it back in your pocket. As he moves away ask him to 'come' and, when he gets to you, give him his treat. This will help him learn that acting right away gets the reward.

USING A CLICKER

Clicker training is useful when you want to mark the correct behavior of your puppy at the exact moment that he starts to respond. If you are doing click-reward then it must always be followed by a reward, but the reward and the timing of the reward varies.

In the beginning, all you need to do is get your puppy used to the click-reward (at the start you will use a treat). Keep repeating click-treat. He doesn't have to do anything at this stage as you are just getting him used to the clicker marker which means a reward is coming.

Slowly reduce the time between the click and the treat and vary the gaps - he will still expect the treat and he will know that it is coming, but that it might not happen right away.

Once he gets good at this, you will be able to click without the treat, and vary the reinforcement by using his favorite toy or a quick game that he likes.

For example, when you call his name and he begins to start coming towards you, you can click so that he knows a reward is coming. It helps to keep him motivated to come all the way back to you in the expectation of a good time when he gets there.

Below is how clicker training fits in to the training as well as how it fit in to recall. If you are training without a clicker just ignore the click-marker.

Recall Summary with the Clicker

The general process for recall training is as follows:

1. Call your dog (use your 'come' cue)
2. When he comes ask his to "Sit" (cue). Take his collar and praise his and reward
3. Release his "Ok Go" (cue)

If you are using a clicker as a marker then the complete process would look like this:

1. Get your puppy to come to you. Start by throwing a treat away from you then throw a treat at your feet. Reward every time your puppy comes back to you for any reason. You can add the click with your clicker to mark as soon as he turns towards you.

2. Add a cue . As your puppy turns towards you, again, this is for any reason, add your recall cue and your click (if you are using a clicker to mark or capture the behavior). The recall cue can be 'come', 'here' or a whistle - either your own whistle or use a plastic one.

3. As you are walking on the leash vary the length. Every time he looks towards you, click and then add the recall cue (and don't forget the reward). Practice at different locations and over different distances before you move to the next step.

4. You will now cue him to look and come to you. With your puppy walking in front of you say (or whistle) your cue, as he turns towards you add the click marker. Practice by varying the distance and the speed the dog is moving away. When he returns to you reward.

5. If you want to add a sit then this is when you will add it to your training. When he arrives back to you use your sit cue to get him to sit. As soon as he sits add a click and then the reward.

6. Add a collar hold. You can train this separately or you can add it into the recall process here. When he has arrived back and sits, lean in and take hold of his collar - as you do this use your clicker to mark then reward.

Once he is good and is succeeding with steps 1 to 6 you can start adding in distractions.

You will start with low-level distractions and build them up to higher-value distractions.

Distractions might be kibble, bread, eggs, cheese, meat, and toys (again in order of least to most favorite).

As he moves towards the distraction e.g., the bread, start your recall cue, and the reward process above (if you are using a clicker just add the click marker). If he fails then reduce the value of the distraction you are tempting him with until he is succeeding.

In terms of what other distractions might be, it doesn't need to be his favourite treats but they are a good place to start. You can then add a dog he knows, a dog he doesn't know (high-value distraction), someone he knows, a group of people, a jogger, a bicycle, an old scent, and the high-value new scent (a squirrel that you have noticed running up a tree).

Try and remember to complete a sequence. Try to always have your dog notice you (click), come to you (encouragement), arrive (treat), sit (treat), collar hold (treat), 'go play' (reward). This is much more rewarding than 'come', treat, end of the game.

By continuing to reward after he comes back to you, by rewarding the sit, collar hold and then releasing with a 'go play' cue, he will have the expectation of more exciting things to come than if the rewards ended with the return cue only.

He also knows that he can return to playing if he comes back to you and also receives all of his rewards. Don't forget that the 'go play' cue is a reward in itself.

This will become even more useful once you start going outdoors to parks and longer walks where there are even more exciting distractions and ones that you are not in control of.

PROOFING

Proofing is when you want to 'prove' that the training has worked and you will need to do this before you let your puppy off-leash.

To do this, you will create distractions and then aim to get his to come to you on cue as you have done above but you are testing once more.

Try and arrange a play-date with at least one other dog and then while he is playing with it (and still on the long-line) call him to you. Make sure you have a very tasty treat and be full of praise when he comes to you.

Once he comes to you and receives his reward he is then

released to the cue, such as 'let's go', to play again. As already mentioned, this particular activity is also useful to teach him that coming to you doesn't mean the end of the playtime.

The last step is to practice off-leash - again, you will do this in a space that is enclosed and where he will be safe. Simply let him wander away from you and then call him to you using your cue. Be exciting and have a treat ready for him.

Don't keep repeating the cue if he doesn't come and don't raise your voice to a shout (or scream). This will confuse him and he won't be able to understand what his cue word is. If you raise your voice, he won't think that coming to you is going to be lots of fun, and he won't want to come at all.

If he isn't coming to you as you go through all the training then go back to the long line until you are sure he understands what you are asking him to do.

EMERGENCY STOP

Training for an emergency stop can save your dog's life. It is also quite easy to train especially once you have been working on recall training.

First of all, you will want to use a specific cue. This can be any word but, again, it can only have one meaning. The most common word that is used is 'Stop'.

To begin with, have your puppy sitting in front of you and have a treat in your hand. If your puppy is not food orientated try using one of his toys.

Take a step back, put your arm in the air as if you are trying to stop the traffic or saying hello to someone who is a distance away. This is important as it is more likely that your emergency stop signal will be visual and not sound-based because your dog is more likely to be a distance away from you.

Raise your arm with the treat in your hand, say the word 'Stop', and then throw the treat over your dog's head towards his rear so that the treat falls behind him or just beside him. You want to make sure that your dog needs to turn around to get the treat.

As he starts to return to you, repeat by putting your arm in the air, saying 'Stop' and throwing another treat over his head. This will force him to stop to turn around to get the treat.

You will notice that he starts to pay attention to you and your hand, which is what you want him to do.

Once he is paying attention, stopping and turning to get the treat as you raise your arm, you can think about increasing the distance of your throw. If there are any problems with the next step return to this previous stage.

Keep throwing the treat a bit further away so that there is a bigger distance between you both, so that when you say 'Stop', put your arm in the air, and throw the treat over his head, he is not close to you. This is how you can build up the long-distance emergency stop.

Try to make sure the treat doesn't land in front of him because you want him to turn around to get the treat. You want him to do this because it stops his forward movement. Keep building up the distance and repeating the exercise.

You want to reach the point where, with your arm in the air, you say Stop, he looks towards you and stops. If he starts to come towards you, go back to the first step and reinforce the Stop when he is right in front of you.

If your dog is a fast learner it may take a few days but this can take a few weeks so just be patient.

The very last step is when you don't throw the treat at the end but, instead, you walk towards him to give him the reward. This is because, if you are in a park and he is far away, you won't be able to throw a treat behind him but you want him to know that a reward is coming.

RECALL: WHAT NOT TO DO

- If your dog does not return to you when you call him simply go and retrieve him and put him on his leash. Don't be angry with him, simply put him on the leash, and move him away from whatever it is that is distracting him. This, in itself, lets him know that coming back is a much better option.

- Don't keep calling the same cue over and over again. For example, if he does not come when you call and you keep repeating the cue louder and louder the cue itself will lose its value and your puppy will simply tune it out as noise. If your cue isn't working then choose a new one and train your puppy to know what it is.

- Don't have only one person training him if he lives with other family members. If your puppy is a family dog then everyone needs to be involved in the training, and everyone needs to use the same cues. Ideally, everyone should be involved in the daily training, even for just a few minutes.

- Never punish your puppy when he fails. This is particularly important with recall (and with separation anxiety). If you get angry with them, or punish them, when they finally return to you after not coming back right away, all they will learn is that coming back to you is not a good experience and that it has negative consequences. It is not fun. All this will do is make his recall worse, not better.

- Don't use the "come" cue if your dog if fully focused on something else and is unlikely to 'hear' you. In this case, use his name to get his attention and to check that he can hear you (does he react by turning slightly towards you or twitch his ear). If he does, then use his "come" cue. If he is far away, you can use a whistle or whistle yourself, and if he can see you use your hand signal.

- Therefore, only use your "come" cue if you think it is likely to succeed. If you call and he does not come, walk to him. Don't give him into trouble or reward him. If he does not 'come' you know he is not fully trained so re-start the training to the point he was succeeding, and build it up again from there.
- Finally, do no use the recall cue for things they might not like doing. For example, don't associate it with a bath, or getting groomed, or having a tick removed if they don't like these things.

GOING TO THE PARK

⚜

Once you are ready to go to the park you are going to encounter even more distractions and you will want to begin with using high value (or higher value) treats than you have been using indoors and in the enclosed area.

It is going to be harder for him to return, and therefore you want the reward to be extra special. You will also vary these treats so he doesn't know what to expect but he knows a really tasty treat is coming.

You might also want to vary the timing of the treat so he knows it's coming and it will be tasty but it might be in 1, 2, or 5 seconds (you will want to start varying the immediacy of the reward when you are doing the outdoor enclosed training).

Try not to only call your dog to you at the end of his walk. If you do it throughout the walk and reward him each time he comes back, he won't associate recall with the end of playtime.

At the end of the walk, make coming back fun and rewarding rather than something he doesn't like. I tend to play more at the end of the walk as I return to the entry gate of the park.

During the walk, you can vary his treat reward depending on

how well he comes back to you when you give his the recall cue. If you call, and he continues to do what he is doing for a minute or two and then comes back, don't reward him right away. Let him smell his treat and then let him start to move away from you. Call him again quickly (you want him to succeed) and if he immediately turns around and comes back then reward and praise him.

In the early stages, try rewarding him with one of his less favorite treats rather than no reward at all for taking his time to come back. You want to ensure that he doesn't think he is being punished (by not getting his treat) for coming back, even if he took his time about it.

If you have already established a connection with your puppy and he finds you interesting, this will be much easier.

You can take your puppy to the park on a long line but never let him off-leash until you are confident of his recall - even if you have proofed, the first time you take him you will want to start slowly.

You can let go of the long line, and if he runs too far, you can stand on the end of it. It is much easier to do this than try and grab a shorter lead.

As you start to venture out on walks, your puppy won't be the only one meeting other similar animals to talk and play with.

It's important to pay attention to your puppy and to keep playing with him, and being fun, during a walk too. Standing around and talking to other dog walkers and ignoring him will mean, although he might be well exercised by all his running around, he is learning that you are not the most exciting thing in his life and his attention to you (and your recall cue) may not be 'heard'. He will simply tune it out as his attention will be elsewhere.

Other dogs and their communication signals

The first thing that is going to happen when you can take your puppy out for real walks after his required vaccinations, is that he is going to meet lots of new dogs that you both don't know.

Your puppy is going to be playful and excited to meet them, but these dogs may not be so eager to have an excited puppy trying to play with them.

Older dogs (those over 2 years old) are not likely to want to play - in fact - dogs over 2 years old will tend to only play with dogs they know. Many will stop playing with other dogs altogether.

You will also need to pay attention to how the dogs you meet are reacting. Dogs will tell you far in advance if they are getting annoyed, are uncomfortable or feel threatened.

I don't know how many times I have seen the owner of a dog watch as his dog tries to get another dog to play. The dog being approached tries, again and again, to say 'no' until eventually, it runs out of options and snaps or even tries to bite the dog who is pestering it.

These are the general stages to watch out for, and this will be the case both for your dog, and for the dogs that you meet. Try to pay attention to what dogs are telling each other and telling us.

If a dog is displaying this behavior, then these are signs that he is feeling threatened, and is not happy with the attention of another dog: -

Stage 1: Yawning, looking away, licking lips, moving away
Stage 2: Panting, hackles up, and whale eyes (when a dog shows the whites of his eyes). This is a clear warning signal. If this still doesn't work then the next part will be a lip curl or snarl
Stage 3: Lip curl or snarl or growl and possibly a snap. Then finally we will reach the stage we don't want to be
Stage 4: A lunge towards the other dog (or the source of the

'threat') with barking as your dog tries to make the threat go away and then this may be followed by a bite.

How dogs greet each other

You need to be aware of other dogs and understand what they are saying.

A dog running at another dog, especially face-on, is not going to go down well. I am still surprised how often I see dog owners letting their dogs do this. A dog running face-on to your dog is often a sign of dominance.

If you see a dog running towards your puppy or dog, then there are a few things you can do.

As soon you see this happening, and depending on how far away the approaching dog is, and how fast it is running, throw a ball or a stick to distract your dog. This can sometimes encourage the approaching dog. If you notice this, just ignore the other dog and turn away with your own dog in the opposite direction.

In my case, if Barney, for example, is playing further away from me, and he feels threatened by another dog, he comes back to me to be safe. If a dog runs towards him, he comes as close as he can to me. This is what you want your dog to do. You want him to come to you for safety.

Most dogs will always try avoidance if they can.

Other signs to watch out for include tails. Are the tails up, and are the hackles up? Neither necessarily mean that the dog is aggressive but it indicates high adrenaline. If you notice this, distract your puppy or dog away from the other dog.

Two dogs that meet each other head-on and stare into each others faces are not being friendly, but a dog that approaches from the side is being polite and asking for the intrusion into your dog's space.

A face greeting followed by a bottom sniff tends to be friendly. Bottom sniffing, generally, is fine and nothing to worry about.

If a dog puts his head across another dogs' shoulders this can be a sign of aggression and it can often be followed by mounting.

Just remember to always ask the owner of the any dog if it is ok for your puppy or dog to play with their dog. Do this especially if their dog is on a leash. Don't forget a dog that is on a leash might feel threatened by a dog, who is not on a leash, and who then tries to play with them. The dog on the leash will feel constrained, and this can lead to anxiety and a reaction to defend itself.

All of this is very important as your puppy begins his first walks. The experiences he has with new dogs at this stage are vital to how he views other dogs in the future. If his experience is negative, then he can easily build a negative association with dogs he doesn't know - and be aggressive himself because he might see them as a threat.

One of the ways that you can help keep your puppy from getting over-excited around dogs is to be more exciting yourself! Of course, you can also teach him sit-stay.

Every time he sees another dog you will want to get him to sit and stay (and reward and praise him at each stage). You can use a clicker if you wish, and every time he learns a little bit more, click and reward.

As you first start to take your puppy out, he is likely to want to run up to dogs himself. This is very different as it will be clear to most dogs that he is not being aggressive but curious and playful.

However, and as noted earlier, dogs older than 2 years old don't tend to like being harassed by a puppy so just make sure you don't create a situation that then leads your puppy being reprimanded by a dog who does not want to play. This can mean that your puppy learns to fear other dogs.

Millie, who is now 11 years old and has been a mum hisself, will persevere with a puppy for a few minutes but he will then let it know to leave her alone. Barney, who is younger, will try to completely ignore a puppy for as long as he can and then let the puppy know he doesn't like the attention.

However, puppies learn by meeting new dogs, they learn how far they can go and eventually learn not to bother them if they don't want to play. So try and teach your puppy the basics with a dog you know.

How to interact with humans

You will already know some of these but a couple of points are worth re-stating. Don't let a stranger pat your puppy or dog on the head. They can bring their hand slowly towards them from the side so he can sniff the hand.

If your puppy starts to back away this is a sign of fear, and an early communication, so try to notice it and don't ignore it.

If your puppy starts to yawn, or lick his lips, then this is the next level of communication, and he is really trying to tell you and the other person that he is uncomfortable.

The final warning will be a bark. He will only get to this stage if nothing else has worked.

The best way to try and teach him that someone is not to be feared is to reward your puppy when he sees them to create a positive association.

You can also try showing your puppy that there is nothing to fear by touching, perhaps shaking a hand, and quietly talking, and while you are doing this, reward with a high-value treat.

Games

You will use games for lots of reasons. One of the things you want to get your puppy to do is to watch you, and know where you are. You always want to be moving around so that he knows he needs to keep an eye on you all of the time.

Hide and go seek is a great game to play. I love it more than the dogs and you probably will too. This is a fun game that teaches them to pay attention to you. I still play hide and seek with them just to remind them to watch me and know where I am. All you do is hide behind a tree or a wall or any object. Let him run over to you and then come out, praise him and give him his treat. It's really simple but they love it. But make sure that you know where HE is at all times. Don't let him be out of sight.

A good way to play a game that reinforces paying attention to you (and can help remove any anxiety of other dogs that might be close-by) is to have him walk slightly in front of you, and then throw a really nice (and smelly) treat near you both for no apparent reason. This helps your puppy know that you might do something fun when he isn't expecting it.

A game I have found particularly good with my dogs is ball play and most Poodles love to play with a ball. The great thing about throwing a ball is that they always need to come back to you so that you can throw it for them again. For me, it means when I am out with the dogs, they rarely leave me.

Millie moves between balls, sticks and he loves pine cones (in the winter she loves to find a lost glove). They might surprise you with the things they love to retrieve (I call it 'fetch' and use this word as a cue). Frisbees are also popular and we had a retriever who loved a Frisbee.

Another great game is chase. As the name suggests, as your puppy is coming towards you give them lots of praise and get them to chase you. Most dogs love this game but some just don't have any interest in it, so this will depend on your own puppy. But changing up the reward, and keeping things exciting and different for your puppy is really important or they might get bored with you.

Never play chase the other way around. Never chase your puppy or dog as a game. Chasing teaches him the opposite of what you want for recall (and being able to take hold of him, especially if you need to do it quickly). It will be very confusing for him when he doesn't get rewarded when he runs away from you and it can cause all sorts of problems.

Finally, and one last example of a fun game is piggy in the middle. This is a great game for recall and everyone can join in. As the name suggests, someone calls your puppy's name and gives them a treat or a toy, then someone else calls his name and he runs to them and gets a treat or the toy, and so on. This is actually great fun and a great way to get comfortable when you go to the park for the first time.

Your puppy will let you know what games and toys he likes best.

GENERAL TRAINING TIPS

INTRODUCING HIM TO THE SITTER

I f you are going to use a dog sitter or dog walker then, in the beginning, don't take him to the sitter. It is much better if the sitter comes to your house to pick him up. If you take him to the sitter, you have to 'leave' him. If the sitter comes to pick him up then you are 'staying'. Do this until your dog is happy and comfortable with the sitter or walker.

INTRODUCING HIM TO A NEW HOME WITH DOGS

If you are going to visit someone who has dogs then you want to introduce him to the other dogs in a neutral environment. It is better to take them all for a walk before you go into the house so that they can get to know each other first.

ACTIVITIES TO AVOID UNTIL ADULTHOOD

Agility training and obstacle courses, and having too many long walks or runs when they are young is not good for your puppy because his joints are not fully mature.

Doing too much, too early can cause problems in later life especially if there is any risk of hip dysplasia. Wait until they have reached adulthood before you take them running with you or you take them to agility classes. Fetch games and swimming are much better for them when they are younger (but not it they like jumping for the ball every time they play fetch).

EXCESSIVE BARKING

Your dog can bark for a few reasons:

• **Guarding**: At certain times, barking for guarding is the correct behaviour but your Poodle can become overly attached to you and bark at friends and family when they are around you.
• **Offensive/Defensive**: This can happen in the park or if a new dog is introduced to your Poodle. This is most likely because your Poodle is nervous or lacks confidence. They might see these encounters as a threat to their safety and so they bark to scare it away (defensive) or warn of an attack (offensive).
• **Boredom/Attention Seeking**: As we know, Poodles are very intelligent and this means that they can get bored easily and start seeking your attention if you are not focused on them. This can lead to barking and nipping (or chewing). This problem can be reinforced because when they behave like this, they get more attention.
• **Excited**: Poodles can bark when they are excited.

The first step is to identify which reason is causing this behaviour - and it could also be separation anxiety which we discuss in the following chapter.

If the reason is either separation anxiety or boredom and attention seeking then you will focus on the cause. In terms of boredom and attention then the easiest way to deal with this is to give him games to play that can keep his occupied. You want games that test his mind such as getting food out of a Kong or a ball out of a box.

For guarding and offensive/defensive barking, then you want to use positive training to tackle the problem. Whatever you do, don't shout at him to stay quiet because this will make him believe that the 'threat' is even greater.

Try to introduce a safe place for him in the home - a place where he can go to - this can be his basket or his cage. If he starts to bark when someone new is in the home (or when the doorbell rings), you will ignore him until he stops, then you will ask him to go to his 'basket'.

You want to get his attention (deflection) and then give him a reward. You then want to ask him to go to his basket and when he does you need to make a fuss of him and give him a treat. You are aiming to train him to go to his 'safe place' and it may take a few weeks. If he is reacting to visitors in your home, then you might also have the person who is visiting give him a treat.

If he is reacting to other dogs, then deflection is the best way to re-direct his energy. Get his attention by asking his to do something - you are only trying to take his attention away from the other dog.

Give him the ball, or ask him to sit and reward his sit. Don't reward him for simply stopping his barking. You want him to do something that you ask of him, so that he doesn't confuse the reward with the barking you are trying to stop!.

If all of this fails, then believe it or not, teaching him to bark on cue might help. This is because you will ask him to bark and then ask him to 'be quiet'. I have used the cue 'speak' then a reward, then 'quiet' then a reward. It can be a remarkably fast way to insert yourself into his barking and getting him to know that you want it to stop

SEPARATION ANXIETY

Poodles are prone to suffer from separation anxiety and, because of this, it should form a part of all puppy training.

But Poodles are not alone, separation anxiety affects at least 1 in 7 dogs in the United States with some studies reporting it might be as high as 1 in 5.

The very best thing you can do, if you have a new puppy or a newly adopted dog, is to train your pup as soon as you can.

Separation training is not generally top of the training list for new puppy parents - we all know that we need to teach sit, stay, leash and potty training - but we need to add separation training to that list. It is one of the most important training exercises that can ensure that both you and your dog can have a happy life and one that teaches his that it is okay to be home alone.

Separation Anxiety can be a form of separation distress or isolation distress - a milder form of separation anxiety. I use the terms separation anxiety as a general term but it will depend on the depth of the issue for your dog.

It happens when a dog reacts to separation (usually when their 'family' leaves the home) and this results in your dog getting stressed. This stress is released in a variety of ways, from whining and barking, to chewing and destruction, with a few poops in between.

This chapter is not intended for those dogs with serious anxiety problems, but rather as a guide, to help with some of the basic steps to ease your dog's anxiety with separation - and to also explain why they feel the way they do.

Dogs are used to living with others. They are pack animals, and in nature, are never alone. As man's best friend this means their pack includes us, and everyone else we may live within our homes. In its simplest form, being 'separate' is not a natural experience for a dog.

Humans can, and do, live more separately. We are used to it because we need to do things like go to work, we might need to go to school or we just need to go shopping. We are therefore asking our dogs to behave unnaturally. This means that we need to teach them how to live in our world where some form of separation is a necessity.

There are a few theories on why dogs react the way that they do but the most important thing to know is that if they are suffering from any degree of separation anxiety then, for one reason or another, they are getting stressed when you leave and they are being left alone. All we need to do is to help teach them that being alone without you is not to be feared.

DOGS ARE NOT THE SAME

Separation or canine separation anxiety can affect all dogs, although research suggests that dogs are more likely to develop separation behavior problems if they are male, come from a shelter, or are separated from the litter before they are 60 days old.

Interestingly, dogs born at home were more likely to suffer anxiety than those born with a breeder.

Separation anxiety can, and does, occur for other reasons. It also happens to older dogs as well as with puppies.

Dogs that tend to have a high level of alertness, like Poodles, are also thought to have an increased chance of experiencing separation anxiety. However, not all Poodles will develop separation anxiety, it just means that they can be more susceptible to it.

SIGNS OF SEPARATION ANXIETY

Separation anxiety is not a failure on the owner's part. There can be many reasons that a dog reacts like this.

There may have been a change in ownership either from another home or from a shelter, there may have been a house move or a change in the routine of the family, it might be due to divorce or the loss of a family member (usually another dog but it could be a cat or even a family member moving away to school).

For puppy's, it might simply be the first time they have been left alone having been used to being around people all the time.

Dogs may also have had a bad experience - firecrackers, a delivery person, or the noise from trash pick-up. Dogs don't like sudden and unexpected noises and Poodles really don't like sudden noise.

Like anyone, dogs can get more nervous if they are alone. But remember, dogs are not used to dealing with threats alone, they are used to packs who provide safety as well as nurture. If they are already nervous or uncomfortable then they will feel even more vulnerable when they need to deal with these 'threats' alone in their home.

Finally, dogs may be bored. Boredom usually affects young or energetic dogs like Poodles who still don't know what to do when they are left to play - or relax - alone and they will seek out ways to keep themselves entertained. Like chewing furniture - this is also a calming activity - or exploring the trash. Exercise will help with this.

Dogs will do some of these things some of the time. But when they display this behavior some, or most of the time, then it is likely your dog is suffering from some degree of separation anxiety.

When you are away

Dogs will get bored when they are left alone. Your dog will sleep – dogs sleep for between to 10 to 14 hours a day - but he will be awake at various points, and he will be looking for something to do.

He might have a sniff around, have a drink or two, and then look for something else to occupy his mind, his energy, and his time.

Dogs like to put things in their mouth, some things fit in their mouths and some things don't. This means that sometimes the mess you discover on returning home is simply a sign of a bored dog and not necessarily one suffering from anxiety.

This doesn't make the experience of returning home any more pleasant, but exercise will help, and finding toys that he can play with will relieve some of that boredom. Other signs, that are more likely to be separation anxiety, are more obvious.

The first thing I noticed was howling when I left the house. I didn't notice it - one of my neighbors told me that when the dog walker dropped them off after their walk they would howl for quite a while. Until this point, I had no idea.

This not only made me feel like a bad dog parent, but it also made me feel like a bad neighbor.

I would then leave the house for a few minutes and wait outside to see if this was an occasional thing or something they did all the time. Sure enough, after a few minutes, I would hear the howling.

This made it very hard for me to leave the house without worrying about them. Commonly, the signs of distress manifest almost as soon as you leave the house.

Howling or barking is not the only sign of separation anxiety. Other signs include excessive barking, panting or whining, and indoor accidents. This won't be due to not being housebroken.

Stress can result in either peeing or pooping or both. They may also chew things to calm themselves, scratch at doors or windows and some might try to escape.

They are more likely to be scratching the door that you left from, or the window from where they can see you leave, they might chew something that smells of you - a shoe, sock, or even a magazine.

Signs of general stress in dogs will be panting and pacing and this may well be evident in your dog if he is suffering from separation anxiety.

Is your dog panting when you return home? This might be due to whining and barking while you were gone. You will notice this at other times too.

Separation anxiety is not only when you leave the house and the dog is alone. It can also be when dogs become anxious when they are not seated near you or can't see you even if you are still at home.

Does your dog follow you around and want to sit beside you all the time? Does he sit against your legs or feet (this way he will know as soon as you move)?

What happens when you leave? Is it only you that your dog is focused on (if you share your home with family). In some cases, it doesn't matter if he is with another person in the home when you leave - it is specifically you that matters to him.

If you share your home and want to find this out, simply have a friend or family member stay with him (with some treats) and leave the house. How does he react? Does he ignore the treats and look for you and if he does, for how long for? Or does he settle down with the other person and enjoy his treats?

If you are not sure how your dog is reacting when you leave then it is useful to record your dog when you are not there. What does he do when you leave? Does he go to the door for a few minutes - how long? Take note of everything you can see and what he does. This is one of the best ways to find out what is happening when you are gone.

SIGNS OF ANXIETY

Does your dog start to behave differently as you get ready to leave, before you have started to get ready or when you are getting ready to leave? My dogs started to react to me picking up my coat or my car keys. If I was going on a trip - which might only be once every few months, one of my dogs would immediately start to pace around and look 'sad' as soon as I got a suitcase out.

The first thing to do is to take notice of their behavior and try and think about whether it has changed and why it might have changed. What changes have you made, if any?

Notice how much and how often your dog is following you (even if he is a new puppy). If it's an older dog try to think back to any changes - is he sitting beside you more often, following your more than he used to? Is there any other reason or a point in time that you can identify?

The solution to this part of their behavior is to slowly build them up to being comfortable with you not being beside or near them so that they get used to your absence and learn (or re-learn) that you come back.

It is perfectly natural for dogs to show some anxiety - so don't over-react or worry about it. But if they do suffer from anxiety or nervousness, it is more likely they will also suffer from separation anxiety.

Sometimes any or some of the signs can be displayed for other reasons, so if you are worried at all just check with your veterinarian.

PUNISHMENT WON'T WORK

Before we talk about all the things that can be done to help with separation anxiety, it is useful to understand why punishment just won't work.

Have you ever taken your dog over to the 'scene of the crime' and pointed at it? I have done this and we all will have done this or be tempted to do it.

Notice that the dog appears to look guilty and might cower. We, as humans, project our own interpretation onto this behavior, and assume that the dog is noticing what it has done and feels 'guilty' about it.

This is not what is happening. What we see as 'looking guilty' is appeasement behavior. It can be a way that your dog is releasing tension to try and get rid of their fear. The cowering, flat ears and tail between the legs, or looking away, is your dog trying to placate you.

Your dog might know that he has emptied the trash all over the kitchen floor and that he dragged it around the house (and that it was fun), but he won't connect what he has done minutes or hours later to why you are behaving the way that you are towards him.

All your dog will know is that you are not happy with him and he will be fearful. He will try to placate you but he won't know what he has done. No matter how much you point at that mess your dog is not going to know why you are angry with him - and that anger will be scary to him.

To reiterate, dogs won't associate something done hours or

even minutes ago with the here-and-now. No matter how much we tell them, they simply won't understand what is going on with us and why we are making them scared.

This all means that punishment when you return home because you have encountered a mess, will make your dog stressed about you coming home. He will already have been stressed about you leaving, and he will have been stressed while you were away. Punishment when you return home can make any anxiety worse.

Just remember, your dog has not done this to deliberately annoy you nor to 'get back' at you. Dogs just don't think like that. They did it because they were stressed and anxious or bored and they tried to use that pent-up energy.

They might look 'guilty' when you return because they have learned that they got into trouble the last time you came back - so they appease you as soon as you return.

But they are doing this because when you return, they sometimes get punished, and so they react to prevent it as much as they can.

PREPARATION

It's a good idea to get your puppy used to being separated from you when they are young. Even if you don't expect to be away from them often, there will be times when you will need to be.

Teaching your puppy not to fear this absence, and to let them know that they can be relaxed when you are not there, is one of the best things you can do for both your puppy, and for yourself.

If your puppy can get used to being left for short periods when he is young, then he is more likely to grow up feeling relaxed and comfortable when he is left on his own for a period of time or part of the day.

GET HIM USED TO NOT BEING BESIDE YOU

These are all really simple things to do and are obvious once you know them. You will need to do this slowly, teaching them bit by bit over time.

The first 4 basic steps that you need to take are the following ones.

1. Pick the room you want your puppy or dog to be in when you are not in the house. Decide which room this is going to be as early as you can.
2. Once you decide on the location, start getting them used to being in this room - don't wait until the time when you are going to leave the house. Make sure you have left their basked, bed or crate in the same room
3. Spend time with your puppy in this room - you want them to understand it is not a punishment 'place' or a place that is apart from you, but a part of their household. For example if it is the kitchen and his crate is in the kitchen, have him go into the crate while you are also in the kitchen or create an area that you can block off (and have his crate in).
4. Once you have picked the room that you want your puppy to stay in when you leave the house, create a gate to the room or area by making a barrier so that your puppy can still see you. Again, for example, if the crate is in the kitchen, close the door but remain in the kitchen having a coffee or cooking or just reading. As long as he can see you. Remember not to interact with your puppy when he is there - just go about doing things as normal.

If you have a kitchen counter or an island that has a space under it, put the crate there. I saw someone do this recently and their puppy was happy wandering in and out of their crate, or lying happily sleeping as the rest of the household milled around the room. Their crate really was the puppy's happy, safe place.

You are aiming to spend time in this room when you are **not** about to leave, so make sure that you spend time there during the day, or when you are training them, so that this becomes a place that you are a part of too. You want being in this room and apart from you as a part of their normal day ie. there is no stress for them in not being beside you all the time.

To achieve this you need to start the next stage of their training.

Initially you are going to close the gate but remain beside it. Do this for 2 or 3 minutes but, if your dog starts to get stressed, just calmly let them out.

Keep building their confidence and slowly make the time longer. Start moving around and doing other things as you build up the time and distance. At this point, you will always be in sight.

If they start to get anxious just move forward or return to the point when they were comfortable. Once they are comfortable with the distance, start to move out of sight to a different room for a few minutes, and then repeat the process of stretching the time.

Begin by moving to the door of the room.

Then move into another room out of sight (but they will still be able to hear and smell you). Return after a few minutes, and then repeat building up the time as you go along.

Finally, go to the main door and go outside for a few minutes. Once again, repeat the process of increasing the time you are away and check how your dog is reacting.

If you notice any signs of stress or anxiety then go back a couple of steps and begin building up your dog's confidence once again.

Keep the time as short as you need to, it can start with as little as 5 or 10 seconds, and build the time based on your dog's response.

From the very start let the dog know that the place you have chosen is their safe place. Keep all their things in this room and place their bed or crate in here as soon as you can, along with some toys and chews.

If you are using a crate, keep the crate door open - let them get used to going in and out of the crate and choosing to do so.

Get some chew toys for them. Chew toys are good because chewing is calming action (and it's why they chew things they shouldn't). You could also put an item of your clothing in the room so that they can more easily smell you and feel more secure.

A Kong is a great chew toy to use because, as well as the chewing, the fun of getting the treats or food out of the inside of the Kong exercises their mind. Giving your dog a reason to exercise his mind keeps him happily occupied.

Put on some sound - like a radio talk station. Not at a high volume - you only want to muffle any unexpected sounds.

This helps my dogs. I use the television news or a talk radio channel because these shows are unlikely to have sudden noises. Whatever you choose, make it something that you listen to so that they are familiar with it.

Your dog will be paying attention to any noise they hear, so this can help disguise some of the day-to-day noises that might go on outside (or inside) your home. It is useful to do this as soon as you begin the training to get them used to it. .

Try to teach your dog not to follow you all the time in the home. You want him to feel comfortable being in a separate room from you. Don't force this or make him feel stressed about it. You can do this by playing a game with him but you won't be able to do this until you have taught him the 'stay' cue.

Ask him to remain in one room while you move to another, then come back. If he stays where he was, come back and give his a reward. Remember, when you come back not to increase or cause excitement, you want to keep him calm. This can be a great game for your dog and he will enjoy it as much as you enjoy the results of it.

When you are ready to start the next phase of actually leaving the house there are a few more things you can do to keep your dog calm while you are out.

LEAVING AND RETURNING

Start by leaving the house for a minute, 2 minutes, 3 minutes, and so on, and try and return before they are anxious. If you can, then leave for longer and build up to an hour and so on. If you notice they are not comfortable, then go back to the point when they were, and start from there again to gradually build the time.

Aim to build the routine - perhaps a treat as you leave. But don't kiss and cuddle them and make a fuss with gestures and by your comments. Try and make it as normal and calm as possible.

Of everything I did to help with Barney's separation anxiety, this was the single and most effective technique. It seems so simple yet it seemed to (and still does) calm him. I stopped saying goodbye or paying attention when I left. I just put on my coat, made no fuss at all, and left calmly.

Once you start leaving altogether, do so for short periods at the start if you can, and build up the time to 2, 3 and 4 hours. Do everything as normal and as they are now used to - and make sure they have something to play with or to eat.

Ideally, don't leave your dog alone for more than 4 hours. If you can ask a neighbor or a friend to visit - one your dog might know - or a dog walker. If you are able, come home from work for lunch.

You might start to notice that your dog starts to get anxious when you put on your shoes or coat or if you pick up keys or a bag.

If they start to react to these signs then start training them to get used to these things. Put on your shoes or coat or grab your keys but don't leave. Do something else or sit down and relax (or watch the TV). Keep doing this during the day so that they don't associate these actions with your departure.

For example, one of my dogs would start jumping around as soon as I got my boots out. Initially, I put them on in another room, and then I realized I had to be in control of their reaction. I put the boots on then didn't leave.

You can also try body-blocking. I used this with the younger dog who was was more excitable. As soon as he started to get agitated as the boots or coat came out I interrupted his behavior by standing up straight and then asking him to go to his basket. It's important not to be angry - they aren't doing anything wrong - you just want them to do something else so let them know what that is e.g. go to their crate or their basket.

You might need to go back a few paces in the separation training from time-to-time, as you are building their confidence and their sense of 'normal'.

Take this slowly - leave and come back. Build their knowledge and confidence. Having them exercised will help reduce their energy levels so remember to make sure they have had a walk and have been fed. This will make him tired.

You can also try giving them a favorite treat. This might help them associate your departure with something they can look forward to.

Someone I know uses a hollowed-out bone with frozen dog food inside (they put the dog food in the bone then freeze it). You could do the same with a Kong. They then place this in the crate when they go out or Gove it totem a few minutes prior to leaving.

When you return, don't get them excited with happy cries of "hello!". Don't over-excite them, or over-reward them when you come back. Just arrive home and then ignore them for 5 minutes.

You need to make the exit and return very normal and boring rather than any kind of event to be excited about.

Remember, if they have done something wrong on your return don't punish them or shout at them. They won't understand why.

SUMMARY

- Don't make a fuss of your dog when you leave. Don't kiss them and say 'goodbye'.
- Leave calmly.
- Give them their favorite treat as you leave - give them something to chew on.
- Make sure they have been exercised.
- Don't excite them as soon as you return home, wait a few minutes before greeting them.

(These steps were the most effective things that I did to help my dog with separation).

LEAVING WHEN USING A CRATE

When you put your dog in their crate (if you use a crate) before you leave then don't close the door right away. Put them in and wait until they calm down or lie down.

This might take a few minutes or more so do something else and give them time to relax and be calm. Close and open the door a few times if you like, but wait until they lie down before you close the door.

Don't bribe them into the crate with a treat and then immediately shut the door - just take your time, and let them take their time to get

Once they are comfortable in their space and their room then you can start moving away using the methods detailed in the first step.

SOME OTHER USEFUL TIPS

1. Exercise is an important part of curing separation anxiety.

A 2015 study by PLoS One found that dogs with noise sensitivity and separation anxiety had less daily exercise. This suggests that exercise is one of the biggest things you can do to prevent or improve separation anxiety in your dog. You need to make sure your pet gets lots of exercise every day because a tired, happy dog will be less stressed when you leave.

The study also found that dogs that were exercised off-leash were less likely to suffer from separation anxiety or fear around noise. The likely reason for this is that being on a leash, partly on a leash, or running free, has an impact on the amount of exercise a dog has.

2. A dog whines when it starts to get tense or excited - think of as them releasing their energy. Sometimes they whine because they want something - if this is the case, they will make it obvious what they want. If you notice this and the reason is not obvious then try and work out why it might be excited and calm them down before the excitement level rises.

3. If you have multiple household members - try and share the dog equally amongst everyone - so the dog doesn't focus all their attention on one person. If there are more household members to which your dog is attached, then one member can leave and the dog will worry less because he has other family around.

HOW TO FIND A BREEDER

Reputable - or ethical - breeders invest in good quality dog food, they have good veterinary care, they tend to only breed their females up to twice year and they work to established breeding plans. All of this means that they spend more on the care of the dogs which is why the cost will be higher. If you find a breeder and they offer you a low price then you can be pretty sure they are not reputable.

You should expect to be asked questions about the puppy's care and you may be asked to sign a contract that deals with health and should include a return to breeder clause that means you will return the puppy if you can no longer care for him or her.

If you are not quizzed about how you will care for your Poodle puppy then it is likely, no matter how high the cost, that you are not dealing with a reputable breeder.

Other things that can help identify a reputable breeder will be if they have extensive knowledge of their Poodles and their generations, they will ideally work with a vet, undertake health screening, and if you have been on a wait list this is another good sign.

They should also be able to show genetic screening and the lineage of your puppy (which should be extensive).

HOW TO RECOGNISE A PUPPY FARM

When you are buying a puppy, you might not recognise that you're buying from a puppy farm. Many of these types of sellers are experienced and go to extremes to cover up what they really are.

A puppy farm isn't always obvious, so look out for some important signs at each stage of purchasing your puppy.

Advertising

If you see an advert online, check how many other adverts that the seller is running. A puppy farm is more than likely to be advertising more than one litter and may also be advertising different breeds. To check, you can google the number in the advert to find out how often it is being used and for what.

If the advert claims the puppy has been vaccinated and the puppy is under 6 weeks old then this would indicate the advert is from a puppy farm. (Always request written evidence that your puppy and his mother, and if required, both parents, have been vaccinated).

If your puppy comes with a passport (and has been imported), make sure that your puppy is 12 weeks old. They should be this age to qualify for a passport. If there is no passport then it is more likely your puppy has come from a country with poor legislation around puppy farming.

Always make sure that you see the puppy at his home and where he has been born.

Make sure the seller does not have other breeds - most breeders specialize in just one breed and should have a depth of knowledge about Poodles. A puppy farmer will not have the knowledge so be prepared to ask some questions

Make sure that you see the mum and note how the mother reacts to the seller as well as the overall condition of the mum. he should not be wary of the breeder. But also note how he reacts to the puppy. You want to be sure that he is the mother and not another dog that is being presented to you as the mum.

As noted above, the breeder should be asking you lots of questions to make sure you can look after your new puppy. If they are not interested in you and how you will care for the puppy, then they are unlikely to be interested in the puppy's welfare.

Puppy farms often prefer to deal with cash and do not offer refunds or have a no returns policy. You should always seek a puppy contract that lays out the responsibilities and a returns policy.

Health Clearances

A good breeder will show you health clearances for both of your puppy's parents. Health clearances prove that a dog has been tested for, and cleared for, a particular condition. These are the following test that are recommended by the National Breed Club and have been mentioned earlier:
- Hip Evaluation (Miniature and Standard)
- Ophthalmologist Evaluation (Miniature, Standard, and Toy)
- PRA Optigen DNA Test (Miniature and Toy)
- Patella Evaluation (Miniature and Toy)
- Ophthalmologist Evaluation (Miniature, Standard, and Toy)

Health clearances are not issued to dogs younger than 2 years of age. That's because some health problems don't appear until a dog reaches full maturity. For this reason, it's often recommended that dogs not be bred until they are two or three years old.

CONCLUSION

I t is hard to describe what a unique dog the Poodle is. I know and love many breeds but this particular dog stands head and shoulders above all of the dogs I know - and I have two Cocker Spaniels that I love dearly.

If you can spend just a little bit of time training your Poodle, of any type, you will be standing on the head of giants.

Take the time, watch and learn from your Poodle. They have much so teach you. And how they will love you!

I once broke in a horse and I am not sure I can forgive myself. I was told that I had broken its spirit. I no longer think that it is true, and it was a long time ago. We used to train dogs by breaking their spirit too.

I know for sure that if you love a dog, you can't break it's spirit if you train it properly, and that is true today for horses too. Training must be a partnership. Especially a Poodle.

Both dogs and humans have needed each other to survive over hundreds, if not thousands, of years. We have each learned how to do so.

The Poodle, often thought of as a modern fashion accessory

has been on that journey with us. More than many breeds, it has been integral to it. It has lived with us as a hunter, retriever, household companion, it has lived in luxury and in poverty, it has fought with us - but most of all, the Poodle has loved and cared for us - as we have it. Especially the French.

Help your Poodle learn to live with you - he wants to. Take the time to let him know how to. That is what dog training is all about. It is just trying to communicate in a language that can never be a verbal two-way communication. We will never really talk to our dogs. And yet, we do.

Dog training is not about control nor dominance - it is only about finding a language so that we can each provide the love and the life that we both want - the dog and us - for each other.

Take the time, and learn as much from your Poodle as you think they are learning from you. Don't ever be mistaken - they are training us too!

NEED MORE HELP?

I did this and free online workshop on training your dog to become as well-behaved as a service dog. I wanted to check it out.

I loved it and I have decided to add it to end of my book.

The workshop is designed to help "normal" dogs like yours have the same level of calmness, obedience and impulse control as service dogs.

It's being conducted by Dr. Alexa Diaz (one of the top service dog trainers in the U.S.) and Eric Presnall (host of the hit Animal Planet TV show "Who Let the Dogs Out").

The techniques described in the workshop are fairly groundbreaking, and ones that I love - I haven't seen many people talk of these techniques.

This is because it's the first time ever (at least that I know of) that anyone has revealed the techniques used by the service dog training industry to train service dogs.

And more importantly, how any "regular" dog owner can apply the same techniques to train their own dogs to become as well-trained.

It's not a live workshop - it's a pre-recorded workshop, which means that you can watch it at any time.

However, while the workshop is free, I am not sure whether it's going to be online for too long, so please check it out as soon as you can.

Here is the link if you are reading on kindle.

Or you can use this QR code if you have the paperback.

LEAVE A REVIEW

I f you enjoyed this book, I'd really appreciate it if you leave your honest feedback. You can do this by clicking the link to leave a review. I love hearing from my readers, and I personally read every single review.

RESOURCES AND CITATIONS

E. (2015, May 1). *Dogs of Durer*. The Hidden Secrets in Albrecht Durer's Art and Life. http://www.albrechtdurerblog.com/the-dogs-of-durer/

Churchill, K. W. (2022, April). The Great Ones. *The Canine Chronicles*, 150–160. http://www.onlinedigitalpubs.com/publication/?m=2330&i=743244&p=170&id=8717&ver=html5

Braaksma, H. (2022, March 4). *Poodle (Standard)*. Daily Paws. https://www.dailypaws.com/dogs-puppies/dog-breeds/standard-poodle

Alt, K. (2020, August 14). *Am I Ready For A Dog? How To Be A Responsible Dog Owner*. Canine Journal. https://www.canine-journal.com/am-i-ready-for-a-dog

Animal Poison Control. (n.d.). The American Society for the Prevention of Cruelty to Animals® (ASPCA®). https://www.aspca.org/pet-care/animal-poison-control/people-foods-avoid-feeding-your-pets

Answer These 5 Questions to Find the Right Dog For You. (2017, November 2). American Kennel Club.

https://www.akc.org/expert-advice/lifestyle/answer-5-questions-find-right-dog/

Blue Cross For Pets. (n.d.). Blue Cross For Pets. https://www.bluecross.org.uk/advice/dog

SpiritDog Training. (2021, July 14). *Poodle Colors: 12 Amazing Color Variations From Common To Rare.* https://spiritdogtraining.com/breeds/poodle-colors/

Committee on Nutrient Requirements of Dogs and Cats. (2006). Your Dog's Nutritional Needs. Retrieved. (2006). Https://Www.Nap.Edu. https://www.nap.edu/resource/10668/dog_nutrition_final_fix.pdf

Poodles » JaneDogs. (n.d.). Jane Dogs. https://janedogs.com/poodles/

What Size Dog Crate Do You Need? (n.d.). Cooper's Crates (www.Cooperscrates.Com). https://cooperscrates.com/pages/selecting-the-correct-kennel-size

Poodle Puppy Teething and Chewing Problems for All Ages. (n.d.-b). All Poodle Info. http://www.allpoodleinfo.com/poodle-teething-chewing

Your Complete Guide to First-Year Puppy Vaccinations. (2021, February 5). American Kennel Club (Www.Akc.Org). https://www.akc.org/expert-advice/health/puppy-shots-complete-guide

Gibeault, MSc, CPDT, S. (2021, February 3). *How To Teach Your Dog To Sit.* Https://Www.Akc.Org/. https://www.akc.org/expert-advice/training/how-to-teach-your-dog-to-sit/

Madson, MA, CBCC-KA, CPDT-KA, C. (2020, July 25). *How To Teach Your Dog To Come When Called.* Https://Www.Preventivevet.Com/. https://www.preventivevet.com/dogs/how-to-teach-your-dog-to-come-when-called

PetMD Editorial. (2017, April 14). *Inflammatory Skin Disease in Dogs.* PetMD. https://www.petmd.com/dog/conditions/skin/c_dg_sebaceous_adenitis

Recall Training. (n.d.). Https://Www.Doglistener.Co.Uk. https://www.doglistener.co.uk/behavioural/recall_training.shtml

Simply Behaviour. (n.d.). *Simply Behaviour.* Http://Www.Simplybehaviour.Com/. http://www.simplybehaviour.com/

Yin, D. S. (n.d.). *Teaching Rover To Race To You In Cue.* Cattledog Publishing. https://drsophiayin.com/blog/entry/teaching_rover_-to_race_to_you_on_cue/

https://www.thelabradorsite.com/teaching-a-dog-to-heel/

Salonen, M., Sulkama, S., Mikkola, S. *et al. Prevalence, comorbidity, and breed differences in canine anxiety in 13,700 Finnish pet dogs. Sci Rep* **10**, 2962 (2020). https://doi.org/10.1038/s41598-020-59837-z

Barbara L. Sherman, Daniel S. Mills, *Canine Anxieties and Phobias: An Update on Separation Anxiety and Noise Aversions, Veterinary Clinics of North America*: Small Animal Practice, Volume 38, Issue 5, 2008, Pages 1081-1106, ISSN 0195-5616, https://doi.org/10.1016/j.cvsm.2008.04.012

Blue Cross For Pets, Retrieved from https://www.bluecross.org.uk/pet-advice/home-alone-separation-anxiety-dogs

Tiira, Katriina & Lohi, Hannes. (2015). *Early Life Experiences and Exercise Associate with Canine Anxieties. PloS one.* 10. e0141907. 10.1371/journal.pone.0141907. Retrieved from https://www.researchgate.net/publication/283492761_Early_Life_Experiences_and_Exercise_Associate_with_Canine_Anxieties

Dog Psychology 101, https://dogpsychology101.com/

Pet Poison helpline https://www.petpoisonhelpline.com/pet-owners/emergency/

Debra C. Sellon, Katherine Martucci, John R. Wenz, Denis J. Marcellin-Little, Michelle Powers, Kimberley L. Cullen. A survey of risk factors for digit injuries among dogs training and competing in agility events. J Am Vet Med Assoc 2018;252:75-83

The Kennel Club. (n.d.). *Why does my dog eat poop.* Https://Www.Thekennelclub.Org.Uk. https://www.

thekennelclub.org.uk/health-and-dog-care/health/health-and-care/a-z-of-health-and-care-issues/why-does-my-dog-eat-poop/

dogtime.com/dog-breeds/cockapoo. (n.d.). Dogtime.Com. https://dogtime.com/dog-breeds/cockapoo#/slide/1

Debra C. Sellon, Katherine Martucci, John R. Wenz, Denis J. Marcellin-Little, Michelle Powers, Kimberley L. Cullen. (2018). A survey of risk factors for digit injuries among dogs training and competing in agility events. *PubMed: J Am Vet Med Association.* https://doi.org/10.2460/javma.252.1.75

Dew claws. (n.d.). Mill Creek Family Farms. https://www.millcreekfamilyfarms.com/dew-claws

Jennifer L. Manning-Paro. (2020, December). *Canine Front Limb Dewclaw Removal and the Resulting Carpal Injury and Arthritis Risks.* Hands of Grace Animal Massage and Bodywork. https://www.handsofgraceanimalmassageandbodywork.com/blog/canine-front-limb-dewclaw-removal-and-the-resulting-carpal-injury-and-arthritis-risks

The Natural Dog - A Guide to Raw Diet and Health the Natural Way. (n.d.). Rawfed Dogs - The Natural Dog. http://rawfeddogs.org/rawguide

P. (2020, February 2). *A good article on dangerous things for our dogs to ingest.* Poodle Forum. https://www.poodleforum.com/threads/a-good-article-on-dangerous-things-for-our-dogs-to-ingest.185626/

Neff, Mark & Beck, John & Koeman, Julie & Boguslawski, Elissa & Kefene, Lisa & Borgman, Andrew & Ruhe, Alison. (2012). *Partial Deletion of the Sulfate Transporter SLC13A1 Is Associated with an Osteochondrodysplasia in the Miniature Poodle Breed.* PloS one. 7. e51917. 10.1371/journal.pone.0051917.

PetMD Editorial. (2016, April 7). *Degeneration of the Image Forming Part of the Eye in Dogs.* PetMD. https://www.petmd.com/dog/conditions/eyes/c_dg_retinal_degeneration

Made in the USA
Middletown, DE
04 October 2023

40188402R00090